I0081272

Sin

Al
Truesdale

f·

THE FOUNDRY
PUBLISHING®

Cover design: Arthur Cherry
Interior design: Sharon Page

Unless otherwise indicated, all Scripture quotations are from the Revised Standard Version (RSV) of the Bible, copyright © 1946, 1952, and 1971 National Council of the Churches of Christ in the United States of America. Used by permission. All rights reserved worldwide.

The following version of Scripture is in the public domain:

The King James Version (KJV)

The following copyrighted versions of Scripture are used by permission:

The ESV® Bible (The Holy Bible, English Standard Version®), copyright © 2001 by Crossway, a publishing ministry of Good News Publishers. All rights reserved.

The Holy Bible, New International Version® (NIV®). Copyright © 1973, 1978, 1984, 2011 by Biblica, Inc.™ Used by permission of Zondervan. All rights reserved worldwide. www.zondervan.com. The "NIV" and "New International Version" are trademarks registered in the United States Patent and Trademark Office by Biblica, Inc.™

The New King James Version® (NKJV). Copyright © 1982 by Thomas Nelson. All rights reserved.

The New Revised Standard Version Bible (NRSV), copyright © 1989 National Council of the Churches of Christ in the United States of America. All rights reserved worldwide.

Library of Congress Cataloging-in-Publication Data
Names: Truesdale, Albert, 1941- author.
Title: Sin / Al Truesdale.
Description: Kansas City, MO : The Foundry Publishing, [2021] | Series: The Wesleyan theology series | Includes bibliographical references. | Summary: "Al Truesdale undergirds his discussion of sin with the assurance of God's self-giving love in Christ. Not only is sin an offense against God and neighbor, but it is also overcome only by God's redemptive grace working through forgiveness and reconciliation. After articulating the nature of sin, Truesdale guides the reader to an understanding of Christ's victory and the life of holiness"— Provided by publisher.
Identifiers: LCCN 2021041060 (print) | LCCN 2021041061 (ebook) | ISBN 9780834139855 | ISBN 9780834139862 (ebook)
Subjects: LCSH: Sin—Christianity.
Classification: LCC BT715 .T78 2021 (print) | LCC BT715 (ebook) | DDC 241/.3—dc23
LC record available at https://lccn.loc.gov/2021041060
LC ebook record available at https://lccn.loc.gov/2021041061

Contents

Introduction   **5**

1. Who Speaks for God? Jesus or the Pharisees?   9
2. Who Is God?   23
3. Sin: The Sickness unto Death (Part 1)   53
4. Sin: The Sickness unto Death (Part 2)   69
5. Without One Plea: Grace That Takes the Measure of Life   89
6. Released from Perfection / Called to Perfection   105
7. The "Inflated" Elephant in Romans 7   117
8. Sin as Socially Structured   133
9. *Christus Victor?*   157
10. Divine Gift: Forgiveness That Leads to Eternal Life   173

Bibliography   **185**

Introduction

The Flying Wallendas, a family of daredevil stunt performers, traveled with the Ringling Brothers and Barnum & Bailey Circus. Their high-wire acts, performed without a safety net, astonished audiences for decades. On July 18, 1970, Karl Wallenda, father of the family, crossed the Tallulah Gorge in Georgia, United States. It features rocky cliffs up to one thousand feet high. Karl crossed without a safety net. In frozen amazement, people muttered, "It can't be done!"

Discussing the doctrine of sin may remind us of the Flying Wallendas. Courage and balance are imperative. There are many ways to fail and come crashing down. One failure would be to treat God's love as unrestrained permissiveness. Another would be to treat God's holiness as requiring perfection.

In many ways, the topic is too subtle and in some sense too mysterious (2 Thess. 2:7-9) for definitive explanation. Nevertheless, spread beneath our efforts is the safety net of God's self-giving love and grace made known in the crucified and risen Christ. Knowing this does not make sin any less evil or "mysterious." It just assures us that our being made secure in and victorious through Christ does not depend upon perfect knowledge or perfect action (1 Cor. 13:12). Today and forever, Christ's sisters and brothers are secure in him by (responsible) grace, through obedient faith alone, not by perfect knowledge or action.

There has never been a time in church history when the examination of the nature of sin has been unimportant. But in our post-Christian era the examination of sin is particularly urgent. Ours is a highly relativistic age where, for many, sin has undergone an ugly metamorphosis. Instead of being a grave offense against God and one's neighbor that urgently requires repentance, forgiveness, restitution, and reconciliation, sin has been transformed into "mistakes" and "failures of judgment" or into an illness to be "cured" through therapy. This happens when a culture jettisons God from its corporate and individual consciousness. The culture redefines sin in ways that omit divine judgment, moral revulsion, personal accountability and repentance, and restitution and correction. Or maybe in a "godless" world, "sin" is best explained as the tragic fate of human existence, something to be moderated by individual and communal effort.

Christians can fall into this trap. Instead of worshipping the triune God of holy love, God can be treated as an indulgent heavenly grandparent who craves approval from his headstrong and self-defined, or supposedly morally constrained, followers.

Sin is not a stand-alone topic in the Bible. It must always be discussed with reference to God and then with reference to oneself, one's neighbor, and God's creation. Furthermore, sin must be discussed with reference to God the Redeemer, to his amazing grace that works to overcome sin through forgiveness and reconciliation. The devastating effects of sin must be fully exposed. But they need not have the final word in anyone's life, and they will not have the final word in God's creation.

Chapter 1 asks, Who speaks for God (with reference to sin and reconciliation)? We examine the contrast between Jesus and the Pharisees. That immediately raises the question, Who is God? Chapter 2 answers by providing a sketch of the doctrine of God. Chapters 3 and 4 directly discuss the nature of sin as set forth in the Old and New Testaments. Chapter 5 discusses the amazing grace of God, mostly through a character named Ruby Turpin. Chapter 6 examines "perfection" in the New Testament. Chapter 7 examines what many believe to be a biblically warranted restriction on what we can expect God's grace to accomplish. Chapter 8 discusses sin as socially structured. Christ the Victor makes the Bible, the church, the sacraments, Christian discipleship, and Christian mission cohere. Christ the Victor is celebrated in chapter 9. Earlier chapters discuss God's forgiveness. Forgiveness of ourselves and each other is addressed in chapter 10, "Divine Gift: Forgiveness That Leads to Eternal Life."

ONE

Who Speaks for God? Jesus or the Pharisees?

The Pharisees built walls. Jesus removed walls.

The Pharisees were mainly interested in preparing Israel for God's coming kingdom and Israel's restoration. They believed this required purity achievable through strict Torah observance. They were a renewal movement. However, the Gospels present them as actually obstructing God's kingdom as it was arriving in Jesus and being defined by him. They claimed to be God's guardians and representatives. But they misrepresented God as Jesus revealed him. They and Jesus held incompatible visions of God's kingdom.[1] The Pharisees enforced barriers that obstructed people from transparently reaching the God of grace. Jesus said they imposed "heavy burdens, hard to bear" (Matt. 23:4, NRSV) and closed the door to "the kingdom of heaven in people's faces" (v. 13, NIV). And they conspired to put the Messiah (the Anointed One) to death (12:14; Mark 12:1-12). By contrast, "because Jesus knew God to be gracious and

---

1. Matthew's account of the Pharisees must be seen in the light of the "intra-Jewish conflicts of his time which tended towards invective, angry polemic, and hyperbole." N. T. Wright and Michael F. Bird, *The New Testament in Its World* (Grand Rapids: Zondervan Academic, 2019), 598.

forgiving he consorted with those who most needed compassion and forgiveness."[2]

The Pharisees were correct in opposing careless opposition and indifference to God's will. They were correct that God takes sin very seriously. But they thought God is so holy and demanding that he prefers only to keep company with religious achievers such as themselves. God would not waste time on "religious losers."

The Pharisees were *rich* in divine distance, separation, requirements, and judgment, but *poor* in love and grace, forgiveness, and reconciliation.

Some History

During late Second Temple Judaism (ca. 200 BC–AD 70), the Pharisees and Sadducees were the two major Jewish sects.

The Pharisees were laypersons, "for the most part men of the people with no scribal education."[3] They formed part of what social scientists call the non-elite retainer class. They mediated religious functions and requirements to the lower classes and villagers. They monitored a complex system of purity marked by "holy separation" that supposedly made it possible for a holy God to dwell with holy people. Purity was predicated on many interrelated components, including family lineage, diet, and occupation.

The Pharisees opposed Roman presence and influence. They strictly observed the Torah (*halakah*, law, "the path one walks")—especially the oral law. The Torah is preserved in two forms: written and oral. The written Torah constituted the first five books of the Bible (the Pentateuch). The oral law is contained in the *Mishnah*. It was equally binding. Moses, Jews believed, transmitted the oral law to the elders.

2. John V. Taylor, *The Christlike God* (London: SCM Press, 2004), 91.

3. Joachim Jeremias, *Jerusalem in the Time of Jesus* (Philadelphia: Fortress Press, 1969), 246.

They faithfully handed it down through the centuries.[4] The 613 *mitzvot* (commandments) of the oral law constituted a "fence around the Torah."[5]

The Pharisees, Jesus, and the Purity Maps

Jesus and the Pharisees were locked in battle (Matt. 23:13-36; Mark 7:1-15). Jesus opposed the concept of holiness as the strict separation that underlay the purity system. He and the Pharisees disagreed over what makes a person acceptable before God. In Jesus, God's gracious nearness competed with the rigorous separation championed by the Pharisees. The contrast was certain to erupt in conflict.

Scholars refer to the stratified purity system as *purity maps* and *boundary rules*. These rules determined the religious and social status of persons, places, and things; they provided holy paths to follow. If properly observed, the boundary rules could assure purity or holiness. They established clear demarcations between the righteous, the less righteous, and the unrighteous. One should know his or her "place in the purity system at all times."[6]

According to the purity system, holiness equaled wholeness; to be holy was to be whole. People with defective bodies were ranked last. They were less whole and hence less holy. Defective family lineage also impaired wholeness. "One's social status in Israel was ascribed

---

4. The *Mishnah* (repetition) is the first written record of the oral torah. It was committed to writing early in the third century CE. It is composed of six orders: seeds, festival, women, damages, holy things, purities. The oral law contains 613 mitzvot (commandments), as codified by Moses Maimonides in the twelfth century. There are 365 positive and 248 negative mitzvot. "Judaism: The 613 Mitzvot (Commandments)," Jewish Virtual Library, https://www.jewishvirtual library.org/the-613-mitzvot-commandments.

5. The first passage of *Avot* (*Pirkei Avot*, "Ethics of the Fathers"), the *Mishnah*, Tehillim Online, https://tehillim-online.com/ethics-of-the-fathers/chapter-1 /mishnah-1 (accessed August 13, 2021).

6. Jerome H. Neyrey, "The Idea of Purity in Mark's Gospel," University of Notre Dame, https://www3.nd.edu/~jneyrey1/Purity-Mark.html.

through birth and blood. And so one married within one's rank and above, if possible. But one never married below."[7] However, in Jesus's day, "intention and performance" had become more important than descent.[8]

Lepers, blind and lame persons, and menstruating women were religiously unclean; they were not whole. The presence of unclean people in a community (boundary breakers), such as a leper, made the community unclean, impure, and hence lacking in wholeness and holiness. The woman "subject to bleeding for twelve years" who touched Jesus was unclean (Mark 5:25-34, NIV). The woman who had "lived a sinful life" touched Jesus (Luke 7:36-39, NIV). Because he permitted this, he, too, became unclean. More astonishing, one day Jesus and his disciples crossed the Sea of Galilee to the Decapolis, where he encountered a demoniac. In addition to being Gentile territory, the context reeks of uncleanness. The man lives among the dead, he is possessed by a legion of unclean spirits, and a herd of pigs is nearby. Having cast out the demons, Jesus transformed the man into someone "clothed and in his right mind" (Mark 5:15, NRSV; Matt. 8:28-34; Mark 5:1-20; Luke 8:26-39).

Occupations located persons on purity maps. Some trades were "despised." Those who practiced them were exposed to social degradation.[9] Others were "repugnant," such as dung collectors and tanners.[10] Tax collectors and publicans (freelance tax collectors) were banned as "bogus" because they "enriched themselves by dishonesty."[11] Cit-

---

7. Ibid.

8. John H. Elliott, "The Epistle of James in Rhetorical and Social-Scientific Perspective: Holiness-Wholeness and Patterns of Replication," in Jerome H. Neyrey and Eric C. Stewart, eds., *The Social World of the New Testament: Insights and Models* (Peabody, MA: Hendrickson, 2008), 110.

9. Jeremias, *Christlike God*, 303.

10. Ibid., 308.

11. Ibid., 310. See "Despised Trades according to the Mishnah and the Talmud," BYU Studies,

Jesus taught that holiness is an internal matter of the heart, not a rigorous external protection of body surfaces and orifices.

izens of Jericho complained when Jesus went home with Zacchaeus, a chief tax collector (Luke 19:1-10).

Jesus's disregard for boundary rules aroused the Pharisees' anger and opposition. For example, in a frontal challenge to the strict dietary laws, Jesus declared "all foods clean" (Mark 7:19). Jesus taught that holiness is an internal matter of the heart, not a rigorous external protection of body surfaces and orifices.

Jesus largely abandoned the Pharisees' criteria for being God's friend. In deeds and words, Jesus claimed to be inaugurating God's long-awaited kingdom (1:1-8; Luke 4:16-21). Repeatedly, he blessed and included people thought to be at the margins of the purity maps or completely off the scale.

By age thirty, most people among the lower classes suffered from poor sanitation, protein deficiency, internal parasites, rotting teeth, and poor eyesight.[12] Jesus freely and regularly interacted with such people: beggars, swineherds, prostitutes, people with unclean spirits, the poorest day laborers, dung collectors, and even some merchants. His ministry to them fanned opposition and shaped his reputation (Mark 1:28; cf. Matt. 9:10-13; 21:31).[13]

This raises three urgent questions. Who is this violator of the boundary rules? Why did he violate the rules? Who joyfully welcomed Jesus?

Who Is Jesus?

What Did Others Say?

The angel of the Lord who spoke to an apprehensive Joseph about Mary's pregnancy said the child should be

---

http://byustudies.byu.edu/wp-content/uploads/2021/02/3-10.pdf (accessed July 22, 2021).

12. Richard L. Rohrbaugh, "The Social Location of the Markan Audience," in Neyrey and Stewart, *Social World of the New Testament*, 154.

13. Ibid., 150-51.

named "Jesus [Hebr., *Yeshua* (God saves)], because he will save his people from their sins" (Matt. 1:21, NIV). The angel Gabriel told the "troubled" Virgin Mary that the child to be born to her "will be great and will be called the Son of the Most High. The Lord God will give him the throne of his father David, and he will reign over Jacob's descendants forever; his kingdom will never end" (Luke 1:29, 32-33, NIV). In Mary's response, we learn that in Jesus, God the Redeemer will fulfill his promises to Israel and the Gentiles (see 1:46-55). "The advent of Jesus is deeply rooted in the ancient covenant with Abraham and the promise of a Messiah in the lineage of David."[14]

According to Matthew, Jesus is the new Moses, the "prophet like [Moses]" whom Moses promised (Deut. 18:15-16, NIV; cf. Acts 3:22-24).[15] Jesus is the authoritative interpreter of the Torah. He delivers the Sermon on the Mount, the new authoritative meaning of the Law. With authority this new Moses redefined those who are blessed (Matt. 5:1-12; cf. Acts 3:22-24).

Mark commences: "The beginning of the good news [gospel] about Jesus the Messiah, the Son of God" (Mark 1:1, NIV). The inauguration of God's kingdom is "good news," reason for rejoicing. A new age is dawning. Isaiah's "new thing" (Isa. 43:19, NIV) is happening. The authority behind Jesus's proclamation is that he "speaks on behalf of God."[16]

Mark uses messianic titles such as Christ, Teacher, Lord, Son of God, and Son of Man to tell Jews and Gen-

---

14. Paul J. Achtemeier, Joel B. Green, and Marianne M. Thompson, *Introducing the New Testament: Its Literature and Theology* (Grand Rapids: Eerdmans, 2001), 15.

15. On the Mount of Transfiguration, Moses and Elijah appear. God the Father speaks out of a cloud and declares: "This is my beloved Son, with whom I am well pleased; *listen to him*" (Matt. 17:5, emphasis added).

16. Achtemeier, Green, and Thompson, *Introducing the New Testament*, 124.

tiles that in Jesus we encounter God. He is present in all his awesome holiness and power to redeem. He plunders Satan's kingdom. He drives out evil spirits. He heals lepers, deaf mutes, and paralytics. He feeds the multitudes. As God alone could do at the beginning of creation by overcoming primal chaos (Gen. 1:1-4), Jesus does by calming the raging sea, a symbol of chaos that threatens God's creation. The disciples' "amazement" shows they recognized the presence of the Holy One (Mark 6:45-52).

In Luke, by the Holy Spirit, Jesus is conceived in the womb of the Blessed Virgin (Luke 1:35-37). The Holy Spirit pronounces the Father's approval of his Son at his baptism (3:21-22). The Spirit leads Jesus into the wilderness to be tested (4:1-2). Full of the Holy Spirit, Jesus begins his ministry in the "power of the Spirit" (vv. 14-15, NIV), for "the Spirit of the Lord is on [him]" (v. 18).

In the Fourth Gospel, John declares, "In the beginning was the Word, and the Word was with God, and the Word was God. He was with God in the beginning. Through him all things were made; without him nothing was made that has been made" (John 1:1-3, NIV). John's first words are identical to the first words in Genesis (1:1). The opening Greek words (*En archē* [in (the) beginning]) in the Gospel are identical to those used to open the Septuagint (the Greek version of the Old Testament). The Logos who has become flesh was there "in the beginning," in the primal act of creation (John 1:3, NIV).

John saw Christ's glory (Hebr., *kabod* ["weight," "abundance," "honor," "glory," "majesty"—all the qualities that call forth worship and praise]; Gk. *doxa*). He saw the glory of God the "one and only" (v. 14, NIV). Moreover, in the Logos, the majestic presence of God (Exod. 25:8; 29:45-46; Num. 5:3; 35:34) has "tabernacled" among us (John 1:14, author's translation). The glory John saw in Christ is the glory Moses saw on Sinai (Exod. 3:1-6), Isaiah saw in the temple (Isa. 6:1-4, 6), and Ezekiel observed when God abandoned the temple (Ezek. 10:1-19).

The apostle Paul teaches Christ is the very "image [*eikōn*] of the invisible God, the firstborn over all creation. For in him all things were created. . . . He is before all things, and in him all things hold together. . . . God was pleased to have all his fullness [*plērōma*] dwell in him, and through him to reconcile to himself all things, whether things on earth or things in heaven, by making peace through his blood, shed on the cross" (Col. 1:15-20, NIV).

What Does Jesus Say about Himself?

Luke Timothy Johnson observes that what others said about Jesus was not inaccurate, only inadequate. "Jesus alone can adequately name himself."[17] Nathanael identified Jesus as "Son of God" and "king of Israel" (John 1:49, NIV). Jesus goes further: "Truly, truly, I say to you, you will see heaven opened, and the angels of God ascending and descending upon the Son of man" (v. 51). Jacob saw angels "ascending and descending" (Gen. 28:12) and concluded, "How awesome is this place! This is none other than the house of God, and this is the gate of heaven" (v. 17). "In a single deft allusion," Jesus has identified himself as "the Holy Place where humans encounter God, the one who has descended from God and returned to him, and the 'gate' through whom others can go to God" (cf. Gen. 10:7).[18]

Strictly speaking, Jesus does not "bear witness" to himself. "These very works which I am doing, bear me witness that the Father has sent me" (John 5:36; 8:54; 14:10). The words Jesus speaks are words of the Father (5:37-38). The Father bears witness to the Son; the Son, to his Father. Jesus came in his "Father's name" (v. 43; 6:38-39; 7:16-19), a

---

17. Luke Timothy Johnson, *The Writings of the New Testament: An Interpretation* (Minneapolis: Fortress Press, 1986), 481.

18. Ibid., 481-82.

reality to which Moses also bore witness (1:45; 5:46-47; cf. Acts 3:22-24).

When God instructed Moses to return to Egypt and demand the release of all Hebrew slaves, Moses did not rush to accept the assignment. He knew the Hebrews would ask, "What is the name of the God who sent you on such a mission?" So, Moses asks, "What shall I tell them?" (Exod. 3:13, NIV).

God answered, "I AM WHO I AM. This is what you are to say to the Israelites: 'I AM [Hebr., 'ehyeh] has sent me to you'" (3:14, NIV; see also 6:2; Deut. 32:39; Isa. 48:12). God revealed his name because he had heard the cry of oppressed Israelite slaves, not because he wanted to frighten or impress Moses.[19]

The transliterated Hebrew consonants for "I AM" are *YHWH*. They are called the Tetragrammaton (four letters). The meaning is not absolutely clear. The root means "to be." Scholars suggest the name means "I am who I am" or "I will be who I will be" or "he who is." God's name is inseparable from his being. Unlike all contingent created things, God is the source (cause) of his own being. He depends on no other and is not to be compared with any other (Isa. 42:8; 44:6).

It would have been unthinkable for a Jew to use "I AM" to refer to himself. But according to the Gospel of John, a Jewish rabbi named Jesus repeatedly referred to himself as "I am." The Greek version of the Old Testament (the Septuagint) uses two words to translate the divine name, "I AM" (Exod. 3:14): *egō eimi* (I am). In John, Jesus uses "I am" twenty-four times to refer to himself, fifteen of which have predicates. For example, "I am the light of the world" (8:12),

---

19. Asked who God is, Israel's answer is, "Whoever rescued us from Egypt." Robert W. Jenson, *Systematic Theology*, vol. 1, *The Triune God* (Oxford, UK: Oxford University Press, 1997), 44.

"I am the good shepherd" (10:11), and "I am the resurrection and the life" (11:25; cf. 6:35, 41, 48, 51; 8:18, 23; 10:7, 9, 14; 14:6; 15:1, 5). In nine other instances (4:26; 6:20; 8:24, 28, 58; 13:19; 18:5, 6, 8) there is no predicate, just "I am." Jesus told his disciples, "I tell you this now, before it takes place, that when it does take place you may believe that I am [he]" (13:19, NRSV). To top it off, Jesus told his mocking opponents that Abraham had seen him! "Very truly I tell you . . . before Abraham was born, I am!" (8:58, NIV).

Jesus was either "full of grace and truth," as John testifies (1:14, NIV), worthy of worship, or a liar deserving ridicule, rejection, and death. On Good Friday evening, as Jesus was being placed in the tomb, there seemed to be no doubt that he was an imposter. For three days the judgment appeared settled. Jesus had been rejected, shamed, jeered, and abandoned. All God needed was to let Jesus rot like any other dead imposter.

But Easter morning, by the power of the Holy Spirit, almighty God weighed in and raised his "faithful witness" (Rev. 1:5, NIV; Gk. *martys* [martyr]) triumphant over death, hell, sin, and the grave! He confirmed Jesus's witness. On the day of Pentecost, Peter proclaimed, "Be assured of this: God has made this Jesus, whom you crucified, both Lord and Messiah" (Acts 2:36, NIV).

So, who is Jesus? He is the revealer of divine truth and grace. "To put the matter even more strongly," says C. H. Dodd, "Christ is not only the revealer of [divine] truth, He is himself the truth," ultimate reality identified with "a concrete Person known to history."[20] He is the "Alpha and the Omega [beginning and end] . . . who is, and who was, and who is to come, the Almighty" (Rev. 1:8, NIV).

---

20. C. H. Dodd, *The Interpretation of the Fourth Gospel* (Cambridge, UK: Cambridge University Press, 1970), 178.

Who is Jesus? He is the missionary God Incarnate, fulfilling the prophetic promise that one day all the nations will be included in God's family (Isa. 19:16-25). In Jesus, those who once had "no hope" are being "brought near in the blood of Christ" (Eph. 2:12-13). "Jesus is the one," says Christopher Wright, "through whom people of all nations [are being] accepted in God's house of prayer for all nations." Jesus embodies that house "in his own person."[21] He "accomplished the mission of God for all creation."[22]

What Was Jesus Doing?

Jesus was obediently and completely revealing his heavenly Father as the God of infinite love (John 3:16; 5:19-24). All the way to the cross, Jesus's words and actions show that God makes no distinction between loved and not loved. Not once does Jesus tell a sinner, including the thief on the cross (Luke 23:39-43), that he or she is excluded from God's healing and redeeming love. Norman Wirzba is correct: "There is no place or time where God's love does not seek to go." Jesus "explodes all the categories and classifications we use to devise who is 'in' and who is 'out.'"[23]

Jesus faithfully revealed God the Father as the "God of all grace" (1 Pet. 5:10, NIV). All that is true of God must be referenced to Jesus Christ, God's ultimate "clearing house." To "know" Jesus as the Christ is to become a new creation in him (2 Cor. 5:16-21). C. H. Dodd says that in the Gospel of John, knowing God involves "the most intimate union conceivable between God and Man." It is a "dynamic relation" that produces "the effects of an incursion of divine

21. Christopher J. H. Wright, *The Mission of God: Unlocking the Bible's Grand Narrative* (Downers Grove, IL: IVP Academic, 2006), 495.

22. Ibid., 535.

23. Norman Wirzba, *Way of Love: Recovering the Heart of Christianity* (New York: HarperOne, 2016), 3.

energy through which men may speak the words and do the works of God."[24]

The "good news" (Gk., *euangelion*) Jesus preached was news of the arrival of God's kingdom in his person. He is God's *eschaton*, his final explanatory Word, the beginning of the new age, the long-promised new creation.

Who Received Jesus Gladly?

"Now the tax collectors and sinners were all gathering around to hear Jesus. But the Pharisees and the teachers of the law muttered, 'This man welcomes sinners and eats with them'" (Luke 15:1-2, NIV). In Jesus, the God who removes boundaries now makes those formerly excluded part of his new creation, participants in the Messiah. Ethnicity, boundary restrictions, gender, and social status disappear as badges of privilege.

People who were honest about their needs gladly received Jesus. Zacchaeus even climbed a tree to see Jesus (Luke 19:4). Before the day was over, "salvation" had come to the house of Zacchaeus, for Jesus had come "to seek and to save the lost" (vv. 9-10). For those who received Jesus, he forgave their sins, healed their diseases, and turned them into God's reconciled children.

The Lord Jesus breaks down walls that separate God and humankind. He makes it possible to be honest about ourselves. Being open before God in confession accompanied by contrition evidences both faith and love. The psalmist openly asked the Lord to uncover and forgive his "hidden faults" (Ps. 19:12, NIV).

Throughout our examination of sin, we must remember that everything we say is referenced to the God whom, by the Spirit, we meet incarnate in Jesus of Nazareth, in

---

24. Dodd, *Interpretation of the Fourth Gospel*, 197.

whose presence sinners felt graciously and redemptively welcomed.

Who Is God?

TWO

"Sin," says Anglican theologian Fleming Rutledge, "is an exclusively biblical concept."[1] The meaning and awareness of sin is directly dependent upon knowledge and awareness of God. The psalmist, stricken to the bone by his transgressions, confessed, "Against thee, thee only, have I sinned, and done that which is evil in thy sight" (Ps. 51:4).

On August 21, 2017, our neighbors gathered for a total-eclipse party. Our South Carolina Lake Marion area was scheduled for a total eclipse at 2:46 p.m. We ate, waited, and watched as the sky began to darken. Beguiled evening insects began to appear as "night" approached. Sure enough, at the projected time the sun "disappeared," leaving only a slight aura of light around the moon. We say "disappeared" when in fact the sun had gone nowhere. Its splendor had been temporarily obscured by the moon.

In much of our world, especially in the Western Hemisphere, we are experiencing a far more important and alarming eclipse, the eclipse of God. Just as the sun was unaffected by the 2017 solar eclipse, the current eclipse of God has not affected him. The impact is upon us—our knowledge of what it means to be a flourishing human community, consisting of moral and purposeful persons.

---

1. Fleming Rutledge, *The Crucifixion: Understanding the Death of Jesus Christ* (2015; repr., Grand Rapids: Eerdmans, 2017), 174.

When God fades from human consciousness, values, and discourse, the meaning and consciousness of sin either become grossly distorted or disappear altogether. In our day, observes Fleming Rutledge, "the category of sin has been displaced by other categories such as disease, maladjustment, neurosis, deficiency, and addiction."[2] We suffer from a deficit of moral capital that often leaves us too weak to recognize evil for what it is (John 3:19).

French philosopher Paul Ricoeur (1913–2005) described the eclipse of God as "the dereliction of the moderns."[3] Its coming was signaled by historical, intellectual, and moral occurrences. *Secularism* is one name given to this eclipse. *Secularism*—also called "scientism"—differs from *secularity* and *secularization*.

Secularization

Secularization (from Lat., *saecularis* ["living in the world," "pertaining to a generation or age"]) describes the historical process by which the secular is affirmed. Due to historic changes in political and economic philosophy, neither the state nor economics are "religiously" defined. Advancing scientific knowledge has greatly reduced what moderns ascribe to supernatural causes. For example, our knowledge of germs, viruses, and genes explains causes for illness and disease once attributed to supernatural origins. "For various reasons, societal functions that used to be vested in religious institutions have now been differentiated between the latter and other (mostly new or redefined) institutions—church and state, religion and the economy, religion and education, and so forth."[4] A "secular state," for

---

2. Ibid., 167.

3. Paul Ricoeur, *The Symbolism of Evil*, trans. Emerson Buchanan (Boston: Beacon Press, 1967), 57.

4. Peter L. Berger, *The Many Altars of Modernity: Toward a Paradigm for Religion in a Pluralist Age* (Boston: Walter de Gruyter, 2014), x.

example, does not rely upon a particular religion for its "legitimating warrant."[5] Because God is the creator and author of human knowledge, secularity and the Christian faith, instead of being mutually exclusive, are compatible.

It was long assumed increasing secularization would necessitate a decline in religion. That assumption no longer stands unchallenged. Sociologist of religion Peter L. Berger argues that recent history has exploded the prediction. Secularization, he admits, does present a challenge to religious belief. However, "with some exceptions, notably Europe and an international intelligentsia, our world is anything but secular; it is as religious as ever, and in some places more so."[6]

Secularism

Secularism is an ideology, a closed worldview that emerged from the eighteenth-century Age of Enlightenment (or Age of Reason). Philosopher Charles Taylor says the emergence of secularism was marked by movement from a time "when it was virtually impossible not to believe in God, to one in which faith . . . is one human possibility among others."[7] A secularist worldview is naturalistic, self-sufficient; no supernatural causes or agents are required or admitted. A complete account of the world, including morality, can supposedly be obtained by relying exclusively upon the secular or, more specifically, the scientific method.[8] All references to God for understanding the world and for promoting human well-being are rejected. Secularists celebrate the "disappearance" of God as good news

5. David Novak, "Does Natural Law Need Theology?" *First Things* (November 2019): 19-24, 21.

6. Berger, *Many Altars of Modernity*, x.

7. Charles Taylor, *A Secular Age* (Cambridge, MA: Belknap Press of Harvard University Press, 2018), 3.

8. For a sound explanation of secularism and its critique, see Ian G. Barbour, *Nature, Human Nature, and God* (Minneapolis: Fortress Press, 2002), 1-6.

for humans who, supposedly, are now free to become fully human. Peter Berger summarizes secularism: secularist assumptions presumably provide "the only valid form of knowledge; every other discourse, including such as is at the center of most religions, is superstition to be denounced and ejected from the accepted cognitive canon. There are no boundaries to be negotiated, because 'error has no rights'—certainly no right to a separate relevance structure whose boundaries are to be respected."[9]

In the nineteenth and twentieth centuries, secularists increasingly abandoned all efforts to identify any bridge between religion and reason. Secularism became full-throated atheism in the thinking of sociologist Émile Durkheim and philosophers Ludwig Feuerbach, Karl Marx, and Friedrich Nietzsche. Psychologist Sigmund Freud concluded religion is a "universal neurosis" from which humans can be rescued. In what some call a Copernican revolution, *Creator* and *created* exchanged places; humans became the *Creator* and God the *created*.

More recently, the newly minted "new atheists"[10] have appeared. According to them, advances in cognitive, social, and empirical sciences have only fortified the certainty that religion retards human advancement.

Many believe we live in a postmodern era, where the modern hope for human life, ordered by universal norms of moral and social reason, has been abandoned. Postmodern thinkers (anticipated by the sixteenth-century French philosopher Michel de Montaigne, for whom the laws of conscience are but the unrecognized product of social custom) view the modern belief in universal moral norms and ways of reasoning as oppressive, derived from intellectual

---

9. Berger, *Many Altars of Modernity*, 74.

10. The "new atheists" include Sam Harris, Richard Dawkins, Daniel Dennett, and Christopher Hitchens. The new atheists are also known as "brights" or the "brights movement."

and social prejudices that run roughshod over cultures not part of Western elitism. We should flee universal values and seek refuge in autonomy, for there is no universal "meta-narrative" applicable to all persons. Philosopher Alasdair MacIntyre says we now live in a fragmented moral universe. It is as though the universe had exploded, leaving fragments floating through the atmosphere. No one seems to know how they once fit together or how to put them together again.[11] Catholic intellectual Robert Royal compares the builders of our "post-truth" age to the ancient builders of the Tower of Babel. "Once the tower's builders were no longer unified in their pursuit of an illusion, a good number of them probably gave up on the very idea that there was such a thing as truth."[12]

In such a context, no wonder "sin" has largely lost its meaning. Sin is a religious concept that obtains its correct meaning only with reference to God. Unhinged from that point of reference, sin becomes trivial, meaningless, or controlled by shifting human whims. In the "absence" of God, sin can be redefined as "mistakes," "poor social conditioning," "cheat sheets," or "little white lies." All these "definitions" expose the impenetrable darkness Jesus described (John 11:10). Consciences formed without reference to God lose their bearing (cf. Rom. 1:18-32). Loss of moral bearing compounds as religious, moral, and social confusion increases.

Watching humans who accept the eclipse of God wander in confusion is one thing. But watching Christians

---

11. Alasdair MacIntyre, *After Virtue* (Notre Dame, IN: University of Notre Dame Press, 1984), 257.

12. Robert Royal, "Our Tower of Babel," The Catholic Thing, June 3, 2019, https://www.thecatholicthing.org/2019/06/03/our-tower-of-babel/?utm_source=The+Catholic+Thing+Daily&utm_campaign=5272111e67-EMAIL_CAMPAIGN_2018_12_07_01_02_COPY_01&utm_medium=email&utm_term=0_769a14e16a-5272111e67-244109025.

decide what sin is and is not without persistent reference to God is inexcusable. It is not left to us to define sin based upon our own hunches, preferences, cultures, and denominational contexts.

Sin does involve oneself and one's neighbor. But that is not where we begin. We begin by examining who God is. He has revealed himself in Scripture and definitively in the person of Jesus Christ. We must also begin by relying upon normative Christian doctrines such as the Trinity and the humanity of Jesus Christ. The Old and New Testaments, says theologian Robert Jenson, constitute a coherent narrative, a drama, of God making himself known among his people.[13] According to his own plans, wisdom, and time, God decisively revealed himself by coming among us in the person of Jesus of Nazareth. Jesus Christ, God Incarnate, is the key, the norm, the Rosetta stone for the entire Bible (Luke 24:25-27).

God Is One, Holy, Love, and Triune

Consistently, the Bible declares that God reveals himself. He discloses *himself*, not primarily information *about* himself. He does so *freely, fully, and graciously*, not grudgingly, miserly, or coercively. God's *being is not jeopardized by engaging and communing* with his creation. In creative communion, the Creator-Redeemer makes himself *known*. An *unknowable* God would be inaccessible to informed worship, loving covenant, and fatherly response.

A common error when speaking of God is to confuse God's *essence* and *attributes*. The attributes of anything express its essence, but not as separate. The sun is bright. But "brightness" is not its essence. Its essence—a big, spinning sphere of gas and plasma converted into energy—gives off the attribute of brightness. Similarly, God *is* one, holy, love,

---

13. Jenson, *Systematic Theology*, vol. 1, 63-66.

and triune. His essence is faithfully expressed in his attributes. For example, when we speak of God's steadfastness we speak of an attribute of his love and holiness.

We begin with God's essence: holy love and loving holiness. In both, God's being and freedom are manifest. We do not speak of one without the other. God's holiness cannot be understood apart from his love; his love cannot be understood apart from his holiness. Speaking of one without the other might yield a "god," but never the God revealed in the Scriptures and in Jesus of Nazareth. Love and holiness can be individually addressed, but never separated. Treated improperly, God's love easily becomes permissive, indulgent, and manipulative. Treated improperly, God's holiness easily becomes austere, threatening, and legalistic. God *wills* to be God in his creation; his will expresses his *being* as holy love.

God *is* essentially triune—Father, Son, and Holy Spirit. Everything that should be said about God as holy and as love applies without a hint of declension to each person of the Trinity. The one God who is Father, Son, and Holy Spirit is without qualification the God of holy love and loving holiness.

In the Fourth Gospel we learn God *is* spirit (Gk., *pneuma*; Hebr. *rûach*), and those who worship him must "worship in spirit and truth [Gk., *alētheia*]" (John 4:24). God is someone, not something. Speaking of God as spirit recognizes that in radical contrast to all that is finite (flesh [Gk., *sarx*]), mortal, contingent, and perishable, God alone is ultimate reality, absolute being, living, powerful, and alone life giving. The term "spirit" applies to God who *is* Father, Son, and Holy Spirit. In Jesus of Nazareth, this same God "became flesh and dwelt among us" (John 1:14) to graciously give us life—that is, himself—and "power to become children of God" (v. 12).

God Is One

In an ancient Near Eastern context characterized by multiple deities, the Bible declares there is only one God. Beside him there is no other legitimate claimant. Apart from God, everything is "creature." The *Shema* is the most important prayer of Judaism. "Hear, O Israel: The LORD our God is one LORD. . . ." (Deut. 6:4-9; cf. 4:39). The Shema is reaffirmed throughout the Old Testament. The psalmist asks, "Who is like the LORD our God, the One who sits enthroned on high . . . ?" (Ps. 113:5). He answers, "No one." Hebraic-Christian faith confesses God "is," not that God "exists." God is eternal, sovereign, and transcendent. In radical contrast to all things that "exist" as contingent, finite, and temporal, God alone "is." He alone is the *cause* or *source* of his own being (God is *a se* [Lat., "from itself" or "of itself"]), and he *causes to be* and *superintends* all that "exists."

That God is one and is the source of infinite comfort and unity of life. He sets his worshippers free from the divisive tyranny of having to litigate between divine powers and comprehend and placate a hierarchy of deities. He frees us from trying to achieve coherence in a world inherently conflictive in power and values. In Athens the apostle Paul saw an altar dedicated to an "UNKNOWN GOD" (Acts 17:23, NIV). Polytheists can never be sure they have covered all the bases.

Michael Novak points out an often overlooked result and benefit of God being one and intimately engaged in human affairs. Unified meaning, purpose, and direction in history are made possible.[14] The one God makes human wholeness and community possible. He offers a paradigm of coherence for the sciences, for education, and for com-

---

14. Michael Novak, *The Spirit of Democratic Capitalism* (New York: Touchstone, 1982), 50, 73.

munity. It is not accidental and incidental that modern science developed in a monotheistic context.

In Isaiah we hear, "I am the LORD; that is my name! I will not yield my glory to another or my praise to idols" (Isa. 42:8, NIV). "I, even I, am the LORD, and apart from me there is no savior" (43:11, NIV). God shares deity with nothing and with no one (42:8; 45:21-25).

When at the burning bush, Moses asks for God's name, he is asking, "Who are you? What is your nature?" God answers "I AM WHO I AM" (Exod. 3:14, NIV). Yahweh is his name. It expresses God's innermost self, his sole creative activity: "I cause to be what I cause to be" or "I create what I create." "Natural phenomena and historical events have their origin in the will of the God who is Creator and Lord."[15]

God reveals his name in response to the cries of the oppressed. "I have indeed seen the misery of my people in Egypt. I have heard them crying out because of their slave drivers, and I am concerned about their suffering. So I have come down to rescue them from the hand of the Egyptians" (Exod. 3:7-8, NIV; cf. Deut. 26:5-11; Ps. 25:6). "What launched the Hebrew tribes into their distinctive faith," observes John V. Taylor, "was an experience of the impact of rescue."[16] The God who "will be present" is sending Moses. Yahweh is the redeemer God, not simply an exhibitor of frightful power. He seeks fellowship with us and creates the conditions that make fellowship possible. Robert Imbelli suggests that we should meditate upon the triune God as "verb" rather than as "noun." God is fully alive and active.[17] The central paradox or mystery of the Christian faith is that God who *is* (Exod. 3:14) became fully incarnate

---

15. Bernhard W. Anderson, *Understanding the Old Testament*, 3rd ed. (Englewood Cliffs, NJ: Prentice-Hall, 1975), 54.

16. Taylor, *Christlike God*, 76.

17. Robert P. Imbelli, *Rekindling the Christic Imagination* (Collegeville, MN: Liturgical Press, 2014), 40.

in that which *exists*, without ceasing to be the God who *is* (John 1:14-18; Phil. 2:5-11; Col. 1:15-17). God could do this because that which *exists* is in no way alien to him as the Creator and Redeemer (John 1:1-5).

No other "gods" could legitimately lay claim to Israel's allegiance. Other "gods" are never anything more than finite fabrications. No matter their form, and no matter the importance humans assign to them, they can never successfully defend any higher value than fabrication (Ps. 135:15-18; Isa. 44:9-20; Jer. 10:1-5). Therefore, the first commandment is not an arbitrary command; it recognizes the absolute folly of attributing deity and worshipful allegiance to what is essentially and inescapably finite. Doing so is idolatrous, foolish, laughable, and destructive (Jer. 10:14-15). It is *sin*, a wrong way of "being" *before* God *in* God's creation. Israel's choice is absolutely binary: worship the one living God exclusively, or worship what God created (Josh. 24:15). In ridicule, Jeremiah said worshipping idols is like worshipping "scarecrows in a cucumber field" (Jer. 10:5; cf. Ps. 115:3-8; cf. Wisd. of Sol. 13:11-19). Their worshippers live in "confusion," while worshippers of Yahweh will live orderly lives throughout "all eternity" (Isa. 45:16-17). Grand order attends God's singularity, his sovereignty (Pss. 89:1-18; 96:1-6; Isa. 45:18-19).

The Old Testament identifies Israel's chief sin as idolatry. The apostle Paul says God's wrath was revealed against the Gentiles because they "worshiped and served created things rather than the Creator" (Rom. 1:25, NIV).

Old Testament scholar Bernhard Anderson observes that Isaiah lampoons other "deities" as unable to "announce a plan in history and carry it through" (see Isa. 42:5-17; 43:8-13; 44:6-8, 21-23; 44:24-45). The "pathetic" gods of Babylon "have to be loaded on the backs of dumb animals, causing them to strain and stoop under the burden" (see Isa. 46:1). By contrast, the living God faithfully, even sacrificially, carries his people out of exile and into restoration.[18]

The Shema is reaffirmed in the New Testament: "'Love the Lord your God with all your heart and with all your soul and with all your strength and with all your mind'; and, 'Love your neighbor as yourself'" (Luke 10:27, NIV).

Many Corinthian Christians had converted from polytheism. The apostle Paul instructed them: "Although there may be so-called gods in heaven or on earth—as indeed there are many 'gods' and many 'lords'—yet for us there is one God, the Father, from whom are all things and for whom we exist, and one Lord, Jesus Christ, through whom are all things and through whom we exist" (1 Cor. 8:5-6). Paul adapts the Shema by making "Lord" refer to Christ as well as to the Father.

God Is Holy

Extensively and consistently the Bible declares God is holy (Hebr., *qadosh*; Gk., *hagios*). His name, his essence, is holy (Pss. 33:21; 99:2; 103:1; 105:3; 111:9). He is the Holy One of Israel (Pss. 71:22; 80:18; 99:5, 9; Isa. 1:4; 10:20; 54:5; 55:5; 60:9; Jer. 50:29). His people are to be holy because God is holy (Lev. 11:24; 19:2). Old Testament scholar Walter Brueggemann says, "The notion of 'holiness' characterizes what is deepest, most inscrutable, most marvelous, and most demanding in Israel's faith."[19]

"God as holy" is one of the most misunderstood concepts among Christians. God's holiness is commonly understood as his moral perfection. God embodies all pure perfections, including moral perfection. That is how German philosopher Immanuel Kant (1724–1804) explained

---

18. Anderson, *Understanding the Old Testament*, 455.

19. Walter Brueggemann, *Reverberations of Faith: A Theological Handbook of Old Testament Themes* (Louisville, KY: Westminster John Knox Press, 2002), 98.

In the Bible, sin is first a religious problem—a sinister, deceiving, and enslaving power set against God (Rom. 7:8-11; 8:2); it is secondarily a moral problem (Matt. 15:18-19).

God's holiness in his influential 1793 book, *Religion within the Limits of Reason Alone*. God is morally perfect, or completely good, while humans are not. For humans, holiness means acting out of reverence for the moral law. A person is therefore more or less holy, depending upon the extent to which he or she conforms to the moral law. God does this perfectly, but humans, even the most saintly among us, do not. Sin is therefore a failure to obey the moral law. By Kant's standard, increasing in holiness involves making progress toward moral perfection, as seen in God and as perfectly modeled by Jesus.[20]

Kant's understanding of God's holiness as perfectly embodying or fulfilling the moral law is fundamentally flawed. *First*, for Kant "sin" is primarily a "wrong way of doing or acting." It primarily involves morality. But in the Bible, "sin" is first of all a "wrong way of being." It is failure to worship God. It is a twisted rupture of our relationship with God.[21] A "wrong way of acting [idolatry in its many forms]" proceeds from a "wrong way of being [refusal to worship God alone]." In the Bible, sin is first a religious problem—a sinister, deceiving, and enslaving power set against God (Rom. 7:8-11; 8:2); it is secondarily a moral problem (Matt. 15:18-19). *Second*, if God's holiness is that he perfectly conforms to a moral law, then implicitly the moral law transcends God. It in effect becomes "god," a norm to which both God and humans are bound. *Third*, if God's holiness consists of moral perfection, the difference between the morally perfect God and imperfect humans is one of degree, not of kind. And salvation would be the process of overcoming or reducing the distance between God's moral perfection and human imperfection. And although

---

20. Immanuel Kant, "The Christian Religion as a Natural Religion," bk. 4, pt. 1, sec. 1, of *Religion within the Limits of Reason Alone*, 1793, trans. Theodore M. Greene and Hoyt H. Hudson (New York: HarperOne, 2008), 147-48.

21. Rutledge, *Crucifixion*, 183.

Jesus is a perfect model for us, obedience to the moral law would depend primarily on human effort. Achieving holiness would amount to diligently overcoming our moral deficits. Each measure of success would bring us closer to and make us more like God.

Kant's perception of God's holiness and human response plagues much of Christianity. By contrast, according to the New Testament, sin has opened a chasm between God and humans that no human effort can bridge. The apostle Paul expresses God's righteous judgment that all humans, apart from Christ, the new and true Adam, are "in" the old Adam and under sin's cosmic death-bound power (Rom. 1:18-23; 5:6-31; 1 Cor. 15:20-22). We are radically dependent upon the enabling grace of God (Rom. 3:9-26; Gal. 2:15-21; Eph. 2:8-10; Col. 1:21-23). All "boasts" of self-sufficiency only confirm our idolatry, alienation, and bondage (Rom. 3:27-28).

Paul Ricoeur warns when we reduce God to a legislator of the moral law, as Immanuel Kant believed, "then the meaning of sin as spoken of in the Bible is abolished." Sin is divided into innumerable moral transgressions. "The disobedient, faithless and idolatrous heart ceases to be the root of all evil."[22]

The Bible does not tell us God obeys and enforces some eternal moral law. The moral, as applicable to humans, expresses God's character, his holiness, his love, his will. The Torah (Law) is the *way* of the Lord; it is the *way* God *is* and the *way* he wants his people to *be*, in conformity with his own being, his "doing" of himself in creation and redemption. The holy God judges "with justice the cause of the fatherless"; he defends "the rights of the needy" (Jer. 5:28, NIV), not because some moral law requires it, but because he *is* faithful (Hebr., *hesed*) to himself as Holy Love.

---

22. Ricoeur, *Symbolism of Evil*, 62.

Because of God's loving forgiveness, the psalmist is confident he can rest his hope on God's "word" (Ps. 130:5, NIV).

How are we to understand God's holiness? His holiness is his absolute wholly, total otherness—the "infinite qualitative distance," as stated by Søren Kierkegaard, between God the Creator and the human being the creature.[23] No reality compares with him; he is transcendently unique (*sui generis*). He alone is God, in comparison with which there is nothing, including all other so-called gods. The book of Isaiah makes this clear: "To whom then will you compare me, that I should be like him? says the Holy One" (40:25). "I am the LORD, that is my name; my glory I give to no other, nor my praise to graven images" (42:8; see also 40:12-26).[24]

In a highly influential book titled *The Idea of the Holy*, German theologian Rudolf Otto explained God's holiness is not primarily his moral perfection, but his "numinous" (wholly other, transcendent) character as God. God is the "Wholly Other One." No creature of its own resources can appear in God's presence. When Moses approached the burning bush, Yahweh said, "Do not come any closer. . . . Take off your sandals, for the place where you are standing is holy ground" (Exod. 3:5, NIV).

Encounter with the Holy, Otto explained, is characterized by two responses.

The *first* response is *"mysterium tremendum"* (Lat., "tremendous mystery").[25] It is marked by fear, extreme awe, terror (cf. Heb. 12:28; Gk., *deous* ["awe," "fear"]), or being overpowered. One's first impulse is to flee from the Holy

---

23. Søren Kierkegaard, "Training in Christianity," in *A Kierkegaard Anthology*, ed. Robert Bretall (Princeton, NJ: Princeton University Press, 1946), 391.

24. In contrast to surrounding cultures, including Aristotle's God, the "unmoved mover," Yahweh is not part of the world. This understanding of God did not appear beyond the Bible.

25. Rudolf Otto, *The Idea of the Holy*, 1917, trans. John W. Harvey (Oxford, UK: Oxford University Press, 1936; first published 1923), 25-30.

(see God's instructions when he speaks from Mount Sinai [Exod. 19:7-24; cf. Heb. 12:18-21]).

After the death of King Uzziah, who had ruled Judah well for fifty-two years, a distraught Isaiah went into the temple, where, in the context of covenant,[26] he "saw the Lord" (Isa. 6:1, NIV). Like the disciples on the Mount of Transfiguration (Matt. 17:1-8) and John on Patmos (Rev. 1:9-16), Isaiah tried to describe what can never be adequately described. The Lord was

> sitting upon a throne, high and lifted up; and his train [Hebr., *shul* (skirt)] filled the temple. Above him stood the seraphim; each had six wings: with two he covered his face, and with two he covered his feet, and with two he flew. And one called to another and said:
>
> "Holy, holy, holy is the Lord of hosts;
> the whole earth is full of his glory."
>
> And the foundations of the thresholds shook at the voice of him who called, and the house was filled with smoke. (Isa. 6:1-4)

That is a faltering description of God's holiness, his awesome "wholly otherness," not of moral perfection. In the presence of holiness, Isaiah cried out, "Woe is me! For I am lost [Hebr., "utterly undone"]; for I am a man of unclean lips, and I dwell in the midst of a people of unclean lips" (v. 5). "Whenever characters in the Bible come close to divine grace," notes Bishop Robert Barron, "they experience a heightened sense of their own unworthiness."[27]

Isaiah has encountered the Holy God, the true King, "the Lord of hosts. . . . Woe is me!" (vv. 3-5, NIV). This is

---

26. Paul Ricoeur says Isaiah's encounter must be understood in the context of covenant, "which is the all-embracing factor in the Biblical relation between God and man." Ricoeur, *Symbolism of Evil*, 58.

27. Robert Barron, "The Gatherer," ch. 4 in *The Priority of Christ: Toward a Postliberal Catholicism* (Grand Rapids: Brazos Press, 2007), 80, https://www.google.com/books/edition/_/zrdzBQAAQBAJ?hl=en&gbpv=1.

the first response to the Holy—a profound awareness of being creature in the presence of Creator. The mood is one of unapproachability, awareness of uncleanness in God's presence, awe, fear, and the strong impulse to flee. Awareness of defilement, not moral imperfection, causes Isaiah to cry out, "Woe is me! for I am undone" (v. 5, KJV). This is not a chasm that moral achievement can bridge.

The *second* element of holiness (the wholly other) is *fascination* or *attraction*.[28] Just as God's holiness produces awe, creaturely feeling, the impulse to flee, there is at the same time an attraction, an invitation, an intimacy. Otto says the words "love," "mercy," "pity," "comfort," "bliss," "beatitude," and "graciousness" apply.[29] The Thrice-Holy God drew Isaiah to himself. "Then one of the seraphim flew to me with a live coal in his hand, which he had taken with tongs from the altar. With it he touched my mouth and said, 'See, this has touched your lips; your guilt is taken away and your sin atoned for'" (v. 6, NIV). When Ezekiel saw the "likeness of the glory of the LORD," he "fell upon [his] face." Then God told the prophet, "Son of man, stand upon your feet, and I will speak with you" (Ezek. 1:28–2:1).

Overpowering is not the end of the Holy God's presence. He touches the "unclean lips" of "undone" people, tells them to stand up, and redeems them, forgives their sins, and cleanses them. Peter told Jesus, "Go away from me, Lord; I am a sinful man!" Jesus responded, "Don't be afraid; from now on you will fish for people" (Luke 5:8, 10, NIV). The glorious risen Christ told awestricken John, who had collapsed "as though dead," "Fear not, I am the first and the last" (Rev. 1:17). Karl Barth concludes, God "wills to be ours, and He wills that we should be His."[30]

---

28. Otto, *Idea of the Holy*, 31-41.

29. Ibid., 31-32.

30. Karl Barth, *Church Dogmatics*, vol. 2, *The Doctrine of God*, pt. 1 (Edinburgh: T. and T. Clark International, 2004), 274.

The Holy God is no overwhelming bully. He is Redeemer. He comes near in redemption, without ceasing to be the Wholly Other. Catholic theologian Robert Imbelli says that God's holiness includes "awesome majesty and compassionate presence."[31] The book of Psalms celebrates the Holy God, who is also near as the Covenant Maker and Covenant Keeper. Ultimately, the Wholly Other God comes near as Redeemer in Jesus of Nazareth, without ceasing to be the Wholly Other (John 1:14).

The glory (Hebr., *kabod*; Gk., *doxa*) of God (Lev. 9:6, 23; 2 Chron. 7:1; Pss. 63:2; 72:19; Rom. 1:23) is the abundant outward expression, the radiance and splendor, of his holiness. It is, explains C. H. Dodd, "the manifestation of God's being, nature and presence in a manner accessible to human experience"[32] (Matt. 17:1-2; Luke 2:9; Lev. 9:23-24; 1 Sam. 4:19-22). John says, "We have beheld [God's] glory," his expressed holiness. Where? In the "only Son from the Father," who has "made [the Father] known" (John 1:14-18; 11:40; 12:41;[33] 13:32; 17:24). The conclusive manifestation of divine glory, God's eternal majesty, happens on the cross, where God expresses his love for humankind. But God's manifest action is "seen" only by those who have faith. "Such 'seeing' is the *visio Dei* [vision of God] under the conditions of life in time, and the pledge of the ultimate *visio Dei* beyond this life."[34]

In both movements—wholly otherness and nearness—God reveals himself as holy. If either movement is omitted when considering God as holy, Yahweh is no longer the topic.

---

31. Imbelli, *Rekindling the Christic Imagination*, 27.

32. Dodd, *Interpretation of the Fourth Gospel*, 206.

33. Dodd says Jesus is referring to Isaiah's vision in the temple (Isa. 6:1-5). The glory Isaiah saw was a manifestation of the Logos. Ibid., 207.

34. Ibid., 207-8.

In God's wholly otherness while the creation is radically dependent upon him, God is radically independent of the creation as in any way deriving his being from it. From divine love, this Wholly Other One freely goes out from himself to the world as Creator and Redeemer. The whole creation declares he is Immanuel, "God with us" (Isa. 7:14; Matt 1:23; Pss. 19:1-4; 66:1-4).

God is a jealous God (Exod. 20:5; Deut. 4:24; 5:9; 6:15; Josh. 24:19). In human terms, people are jealous when they recognize a competitor who threatens to take their place. That isn't God's jealousy. God is jealous for his name, his singular being as God. He does not "share" deity as the "gods" do (Isa. 48:11). After God says "I am," there is nothing additional about *deity as such* worth saying (Isa. 48:12; Rev. 22:13). All other claimants to deity claim what they cannot support.[35]

New Testament scholar Michael J. Gorman says that God's holiness is most definitively manifested on the cross. Christ's faithful, loving death on the cross is the ultimate holy act. It is the defining manifestation of God's holiness.[36]

God Is Love

By speaking of the Holy God as "attracting" the creature to himself we have begun to speak of God as love, as grace. Karl Barth says that in gracious love, God "meets us, not in spite of, but in and with all the holiness, righteous-

---

35. Robert Jenson says "jealousy" is God's first attribute. Jenson, *Systematic Theology*, vol. 2, *The Works of God* (Oxford, UK: Oxford University Press, 1999), 133-34.

36. Michael J. Gorman, *Inhabiting the Cruciform God: Kenosis, Justification, and Theosis in Paul's Narrative Soteriology* (Grand Rapids: Eerdmans, 2009), 116.

ness [faithfulness to his promises],[37] and wisdom of God. It claims us, cleansing, judging and redeeming us."[38]

Not only does God love, but he *is* love (1 John 4:8). He is the source of love (v. 7). We know God's love by how he loves—eternally in his triune life, and toward us.[39] God faithfully *does* what he *is*, definitively in Jesus of Nazareth. As holy love, God is the Covenant Maker and Covenant Keeper. He is unfailingly faithful to himself and to his promises.

The Old Testament speaks of God's "steadfast" or "loyal" love (Hebr., *hesed* [durability]). "The LORD passed before him, and proclaimed, 'The LORD, the LORD, a God merciful and gracious, slow to anger, and abounding in steadfast love and faithfulness'" (Exod. 34:6). This is true, not because God "is bound by a law external to himself, but by virtue of his free will, his grace." God's love is characterized by "constancy, steadfastness, [and] trustworthiness" (cf. 2 Cor. 1:20).[40] Christ's death on the cross, says Michael Gorman, is the defining act of God's faithfulness to his gracious covenant.[41]

God's holy love is thoroughly self-giving, which is another way of saying God is gracious. The Scriptures consistently display this love. Michael Gorman says that preeminently, it is the kenotic (self-emptying) God of Philippians 2:5-11 who reveals himself as Holy Love, the God who does not demand his rights but surrenders them as the

---

37. A common error is to speak of God's "righteousness" as moral perfection. N. T. Wright corrects this error. God's righteousness should not be confused with moral perfection. Instead, it is God's covenant faithfulness. The covenant includes not only Abraham and Israel but, through Israel, also the whole world. N. T. Wright, *The Day the Revolution Began: Reconsidering the Meaning of Jesus's Crucifixion* (San Francisco: HarperOne, 2016), 303.

38. Barth, *Church Dogmatics*, vol. 2, *Doctrine of God*, pt. 1, 356.

39. God acts graciously not only outwardly toward his creature "but also in Himself from eternity to eternity." Ibid., 357.

40. Anderson, *Understanding the Old Testament*, 288.

41. Gorman, *Inhabiting the Cruciform God*, 116.

ultimate demonstration of his love for others.[42] Karl Barth says that God "reveals His very essence in [the] streaming forth of grace. There is no higher divine being than that of the gracious God, there is no higher divine holiness than that which He shows in being merciful and forgiving sins. For in this action He interposes no less and no other than Himself for us."[43]

In the Bible, not once is God's love expressed in a miserly, grudging manner. He is self-giving love in creation and redemption. He abounds in grace (Rom. 5:20; 6:1; 2 Cor. 9:8) and is "rich in mercy" (Eph. 2:4, NIV). As we shall see, God is and does toward the creation what he is and does in his triune life. The Trinity is a community of self-giving love. The staggering declaration of the Scriptures is that the Holy God gives himself in love to his creation in the same way the Father, Son, and Holy Spirit give themselves to each other.

Equally staggering for human comprehension is that God freely loves, freely gives himself, with no guarantee that his love will be reciprocated. God's love is vulnerable, not because humans impose vulnerability upon him, but because he accepts vulnerability, self-limitation for himself. Humans know of no higher love than a love that invests itself in another for the well-being of the other without dictating love's results, without dictating reciprocation. Søren Kierkegaard explained that God's sovereignty understood as the power to control or dictate is not worthy of God.

---

42. Ibid., 119.

43. Barth, *Church Dogmatics*, vol. 2, *Doctrine of God*, pt. 1, 356. "Any other idea of God, in which He is not yet gracious, or not yet essentially decisively and comprehensively known as gracious, is really, whether it is afformed or denied, a theology of the gods and idols of this world, not of the living and true God" (357).

God, says John V. Taylor, knowingly and willingly "pays the price of love," including the pain of rejection.[44]

According to the New Testament, through all the twists and turns of history, in spite of imponderable failures by Adam and Eve, Israel, and Judah, "When the set time had fully come, God sent his Son, born of a woman, born under the law, to redeem those under the law, that we might receive adoption to sonship" (Gal. 4:4-5, NIV). God has "made known to us in all wisdom and insight the mystery of his will, according to his purpose which he set forth in Christ as a plan for the fulness of time, to unite all things in him, things in heaven and things on earth" (Eph. 1:9-10; 3:5; Col. 1:25-26).

How did God accomplish this? "In love," the apostle Paul answers (Eph. 1:5). The very life of God, C. H. Dodd observes, "is the outpouring of love." God's love "is a radically personal form of life, manifested in the concrete activity of Christ in laying down His life for His friends."[45] God's love is "not of this world," but it "plants its feet firmly in this world." The "crucial act of ἀγάπη [agapē (love)] was actually performed in history, on an April day about A.D. 30, at a supper-table in Jerusalem, in a garden across the Kidron Valley, in the headquarters of Pontius Pilate, and on a Roman cross at Golgotha."[46] It was this love that caused Christ Jesus, who "though he was in the form of God," not to "count equality with God a thing to be grasped," but to empty himself and obediently take the "form of a servant" (Phil. 2:5-7).

N. T. Wright says that the gospel of Jesus Christ invites us to see that God's powerful self-giving love shown on the cross is the same power that created the world.

---

44. Taylor, *Christlike God*, 164.
45. Dodd, *Interpretation of the Fourth Gospel*, 197.
46. Ibid., 200.

Now God's power is at work recreating it.[47] That is why the cross of Christ contains such life-transforming power, then and now.[48] The power of divine self-giving love has been unleashed "into the world" for everyone. It is "the chain-breaking, idol-smashing, sin-abandoning power called 'forgiveness,' called 'utter graciousness,' called Jesus."[49]

Some forms of Christian theology completely reject what Wright says. They deny belief in the power of God as self-giving, vulnerable, and indiscriminate love. According to them, God does love, but discriminately. He controls its outcome from beginning to end. God predestines who will receive his love. There is no danger it will not be recipro-cated. God's grace will be "effectual," guaranteed by his sovereign power.

But N. T. Wright explains that even if the power that wins by force, by dictation, is divine force or power, it remains coercive. It would not be a winning love. At the center of God's victory over this world's dark powers there stands self-giving love. God in Christ gave himself as a ran-som for many. This, says Wright, is the meaning and center of the revolution God inaugurated on Good Friday.[50]

Love and God's Wrath

The Bible speaks of God's wrath (Exod. 15:7; Lev. 9:6, 23; Isa. 9:19; Hos. 5:10; Rom. 1:18; Heb. 12:29; Rev. 6:16). But how can the God who is Holy Love also be a God who expresses wrath? Many think of God as a wrathful deity giv-en to whimsical outbreaks of devastating anger unleashed against humans. Maybe the wrath of God is a primitive concept that needs to be abandoned, now that Jesus has perfectly revealed God's love.

---

47. Wright, *Day the Revolution Began*, 198-99.
48. Ibid., 199.
49. Ibid., 395.
50. Ibid., 222.

Nothing could be further from the truth. The wrath of God is the Holy One opposing creaturely efforts to stand against him, misrepresent him, or displace him. Jeremiah says the wrath of God is going to break like a fierce storm upon the prophets who have, in God's name, habitually lied to the people of Jerusalem (Jer. 23:16-22). By using the Babylonians as his instrument of punishment, God will pour out his wrath upon Jerusalem's inhabitants who have turned their rooftops into shrines for worshipping other gods (32:26-32).

The wrath of God is God's holiness reminding idolaters, and imposters who attempt to supplant him or derail his plans, that he neither shares his glory with another nor gives his praise to idols (Isa. 42:8). And lest we think the New Testament leaves behind the wrath of holy love, listen to Jesus: "I came to cast fire upon the earth; and would that it were already kindled! I have a baptism to be baptized with; and how I am constrained until it is accomplished! Do you think that I have come to give peace on earth? No, I tell you, but rather division" (Luke 12:49-51).

God's wrath is holy love and loving holiness judging all that opposes holy love (Rom. 1:18). It is an inseparable aspect of his love. Were God not wrathful in this way, were he to indulge idolatry and betrayal, he would not be God. God's wrath and his love are in no way incommensurate. God will either be capable of wrath or incapable of being God. Paul Ricoeur is helpful: "Wrath is the countenance of Holiness for sinful man." It doesn't mean that God is wicked.[51]

Love as Longsuffering

If God were wantonly to vent his holy wrath against all that oppose holy love, his fallen creation would cease to exist. The Bible speaks of God being "longsuffering" (2 Pet.

---

51. Ricoeur, *Symbolism of Evil*, 63.

3:9; Eph. 4:2, KJV), of his forbearance (Rom. 3:25), of his seeking ways to redeem the unworthy and to turn enemies into faithful worshippers. He promised if the Babylonian exiles would repent of their sins—turn their faces, not their backs, to him—he would "rejoice in doing them good . . . with all [his] heart and soul" (Jer. 32:33, 41, NIV).

On the cross, the long-suffering God himself became our means of reconciliation (1 Cor. 1:18-25, 30). There, God unloaded upon himself his holy wrath, his judgment against sin.[52] In love, God punished sin in his own person, in the flesh of his own Son (John 3:16). "What the law was powerless to do because it was weakened by the flesh, God did by sending his own Son in the likeness of sinful flesh to be a sin offering. And so he condemned sin in the flesh, in order that the righteous requirement of the law might be fully met in us, who do not live according to the flesh but according to the Spirit" (Rom. 8:3-4, NIV; 3:21-26; 5:6-11). The living God himself, incarnate in Jesus Messiah, took upon himself the consequences of Israel's idolatry and that of the whole human race. There, in the power of costly divine forgiveness, Paul says, God "disarmed the principalities and powers and made a public example of them, triumphing over them in [Christ]" (Col. 2:15).

God Is Triune

The One God is eternally triune—Father, Son, and Holy Spirit. God can truly be spoken of only as triune. Christians who omit the Trinity when trying to compare God with the "God" spoken of by Muslims are speaking of a deity of their making, not the triune God who *is* Father, Son, and Holy Spirit. Confession that God is triune is absolutely essential for Christian faith and discipleship, not, as Swiss psychiatrist

---

52. In the passion and death of Christ in which he is glorified, judgment of the world happens (John 12:31).

Carl Jung maintained, "a mere object of belief."[53] "Take out of the Christian consciousness the thoughts and affections that relate to the Father, the Son, and the Holy Spirit," says William Shedd, "and there is no Christian consciousness left."[54] Our prayers are triune: they are addressed *to* the Father, *through* the Son, and *by* the Holy Spirit.

Augustine of Hippo (AD 354–430) summarized the doctrine of the Trinity: "All those Catholic expounders of the divine Scriptures . . . who have written before me concerning the Trinity, Who is God, have purposed to teach, according to the Scriptures, this doctrine, that the Father, and the Son, and the Holy Spirit intimate a divine unity of one and the same substance in an indivisible equality; and therefore that they are not three Gods, but one God."[55]

Under the guidance of the Holy Spirit, the early church developed the doctrine of the Trinity in its first two Ecumenical Councils. In AD 325, the Council of Nicaea, against the Arians, who taught that the Son is God's first creature, affirmed the deity of the Son. The Nicene Creed affirms the Son is of the same *ousia* (Gk., "substance," "essence," "nature") as the Father.

In the First Council of Constantinople (AD 381) the church affirmed the full deity of the Holy Spirit, equal in deity with the Father and the Son.

As important as the councils are, affirmation of the Trinity resides primarily in the Scriptures. The disclosure of

---

53. C. G. Jung, *The Archetypes and the Collective Unconscious*, vol. 9 (pt. 1) of *The Collected Works of C. G. Jung* (Princeton, NJ: Princeton University Press, 1981), 8.

54. William G. T. Shedd, introductory essay to *On the Holy Trinity*, by Augustine, in vol. 3 of *Nicene and Post-Nicene Fathers* (series I), ed. Philip Schaff (reprint of 1887 edition), 17, Christian Classic Ethereal Library (CCEL), https://www.ccel.org/ccel/schaff/npnf103.pdf.

55. Augustine, *On the Holy Trinity*, bk. 1, ch. 4, sec. 7, in vol. 3 of *Nicene and Post-Nicene Fathers* (series I), ed. Philip Schaff (reprint of 1887 edition), CCEL, https://www.ccel.org/ccel/schaff/npnf103.pdf.

the Trinity begins in the Old Testament and expands in the New Testament. New Testament scholar Michael J. Gorman says that Paul was so certain that Christ is God's self-revelation that he assigns to Christ the biblical title "Lord." Paul's certainty derives from his experience of the Holy Spirit calling him and others to encounter God's glory in the Son.[56]

Robert Jenson speaks of "the Trinitarian logic of the New Testament."[57] Throughout the Scriptures, but definitively in the New Testament, the Trinity is affirmed not so much in "conceptual" language as the creeds employ, but "in the logic they display."[58] Repeatedly in the New Testament "God" refers *interchangeably* without *qualification* or *gradation* to Father, Son, and Holy Spirit (Rom. 1:1-4; 5:1-5; 8:1-20; 10:9; 14:17-18; 15:16; 2 Cor. 1:21-22; Eph. 5:18-20; 2 Tim. 4:1; Jude vv. 20-21; Rev. 1:4-5; 4:2; 5:6).

Catholic Karl Rahner puts things in order: "We can really grasp the content of the doctrine of the Trinity only by going back to the history of salvation and of grace, to our experience of Jesus and of the Spirit of God, who operates in us, because in them we really already possess the Trinity itself as such."[59] The Trinity, Rahner adds, is not primarily a doctrine. "The Trinity itself is with us . . . the reality of which is bestowed upon us."[60]

Theologians discuss whether there is a difference between the *immanent Trinity* (God as he is known to himself prior to revelation) and the *economic Trinity* (triune life as revealed in time). Theologian Karl Rahner famously taught that "the 'economic' Trinity is the 'immanent' Trinity and the 'immanent' Trinity is the 'economic' Trinity."[61] This

---

56. Gorman, *Inhabiting the Cruciform God*, 120.

57. Jenson, *Systematic Theology*, vol. 1, 90-93.

58. Ibid., 91.

59. Karl Rahner, *The Trinity* (New York: Herder and Herder, 1970), 40.

60. Ibid., 39.

61. Ibid., 22.

means that the mystery of God in himself is the mystery of grace—one mystery. The immanent Trinity is not an abstraction.[62]

While fully affirming the Trinity, theologians have often disagreed over how best to speak of the three "persons" in the Trinity. The danger is that by speaking of "three persons," it will appear we are speaking of three independent centers of identity and consciousness, and hence of slipping into tritheism.[63] One way to avoid this error was developed by the fourth-century Cappadocian Fathers: Basil the Great (ca. AD 330-79), Gregory of Nyssa (ca. AD 335–ca. AD 394), and Gregory of Nazianzus (ca. AD 329–ca. AD 389). They taught that "God" is the substance ("essence" [ousia]) or property common to each person. In each, Godhead is complete. This is similar to saying "human" and then saying Peter is human, John is human, and Andrew is human. There are distinctions in "person" (Gk., hypostasis) but not in "substance." One essence subsists in three persons (with individuating characteristics). No analogy for the Trinity is perfect. The Trinity is "mystery," and why not? Confessing the Trinity is essential for Christian faith; fully understanding the Trinity is not. All efforts to explain the Trinity, as important as they are, should end in worship, not in exhaustive satisfaction.

It is very important to remember that wherever God acts, the whole of God acts. The persons of the Trinity are *distinguishable* but not *divisible*. The author of Hebrews beautifully expresses this: through the Holy Spirit, Christ "offered himself without blemish" to his Father (Heb. 9:14). So we confess *from* or *of* the Father, *through* the Son, and *in* or *by* the Holy Spirit. The one triune God is Creator and

---

62. Ibid., 3.

63. We should not to think of the Trinity as a fourth entity that transcends Father, Son, and Holy Spirit. That would amount to creating another God. The Trinity *is* Father, Son, and Holy Spirit.

Redeemer. The Cappadocian Fathers established a rule that guides Christian understanding and speech: "All action that impacts the creature from God . . . begins with the Father and is actual through the Son and is perfected in the Holy Spirit."[64] We speak of "offices" of the persons as noted in the New Testament, but never of the Father, Son, or Spirit as acting in the absence of the other (Luke 4:1-2, 18-19; John 16:4b-11; 17:6-8; Eph. 2:17-18; Heb. 8:11-14). Ambrose of Milan (AD 339-97) explained that if we lessen the importance of the Father, Son, or Spirit, "the whole mystery is made empty."[65] "The mystery of the Trinity," says Karl Rahner, "is for us a mystery of salvation, and why we meet it wherever our salvation is considered."[66]

The Greek term *perichōrēsis* (from two Greek words: *peri* [around] and *choreia* [dance]) is often used to describe that internal relationship within the Trinity. The term describes the mutual self-giving of each person to the other. It means co-indwelling, co-inhering, and mutual interpenetration, all while maintaining the triune distinctions of Father, Son, and Spirit. In triune life, says Orthodox theologian Kallistos Ware, there is an "unceasing movement of mutual love."[67] Each person of the Trinity shares in the life of the other two. *Perichōrēsis* probably comes as close to articulating the triune "community" as any term can. The most important thing to remember is that the relationship is one of holy, mutually self-giving love.

The second article of the Nicene Creed affirms the Son is "begotten, not made." Eastern and Western Christianity

---

64. Gregory of Nyssa, as quoted by Jenson, *Systematic Theology*, vol. 1, 110.

65. Ambrose, *On The Holy Spirit*, bk. 1, ch. 3, sec. 42, in vol. 10 of *Nicene and Post-Nicene Fathers* (series II), ed. Philip Schaff and Henry Wace (reprint of 1896 edition), CCEL, https://ccel.org/ccel/s/schaff/npnf210/cache/npnf210.pdf.

66. Rahner, *Trinity*, 21.

67. Kallistos Ware, *The Orthodox Way* (Crestwood, NY: St. Vladimir's Seminary Press, 1979), 27.

confess the Son is "eternally *begotten* of the Father." They affirm the Holy Spirit *"proceeds"* (art. 8). But they disagree at one critical point. The Eastern church affirms that the Holy Spirit "proceeds" from the Father only; the Western church, that he "proceeds from the Father and the Son." "And the Son" was added to the Western affirmation early in the fifth century. The controversy associated with this difference is known as the Filioque (and from the Son) Controversy. It contributed to the AD 1054 division between East and West.

Sometimes Christians erroneously speak of God, Son, and Holy Spirit. Without intending to do so, they thereby deny the Trinity. There is one God who *is* God the Father, God the Son, and God the Holy Spirit. We should speak that way. In the New Testament there is clearly a primacy of the Father. But it is not a temporal or substantial primacy. No person of the Trinity is more God than the other.

Conclusion

We have seen how knowledge of what it means to be a sinner begins not by referring to the sinner but by referring to God, against whom sin is primarily committed. Not until the triune God who is Holy Love is "seen" can sin be "seen" as it is. Our secularized world reveals neither. First, all our admirable Uzziahs must die, our temple foundations shaken, and our unclean lips cleansed (Isa. 6:1-5).

THREE

Sin
The Sickness unto Death (Part 1)

It is as if an author were to make a slip of the pen. Then the slip would become conscious of itself, but in a far higher sense, as an essential constituent in the whole exposition. Then it would revolt against its Author and, in resentment, forbid the Author to make a correction. To the Author it would say: "No, I will not be corrected. I will stand as a witness against Thee. Thou art a very poor writer!"

—Søren Kierkegaard, "The Sickness unto Death"[1]

In this chapter we discuss the following: (1) Jesus reveals sin; (2) knowledge of sin; (3) sin as a powerful, ubiquitous kingdom; and (4) the kingdom of evil converges.

Chapter 4 will consider (1) how the Old Testament understands sin, (2) how the New Testament understands sin, and (3) sin against the creation.

Three convictions or assumptions underlie a biblical and Christian treatment of sin. *First,* there is the reality of an "original" departure by humankind from the will of God. Cardinal John Henry Newman labeled it a "terrible

---

1. Søren Kierkegaard, "The Sickness unto Death," in *A Kierkegaard Anthology,* ed. Robert Bretall (Princeton, NJ: Princeton University Press, 1946), 371, paraphrased; change of capitalization intended.

aboriginal calamity."[2] *Second,* the departure is evidenced and experienced in human solidarity—individually and corporately—as bondage to sin (Rom. 7:24). *Third,* a forceful cosmic alliance or kingdom composed of sin, evil, and death (the world, the flesh, and the devil) (Acts 26:18; 2 Cor. 4:4; Eph. 2:2; Col. 1:13) exists. This alliance, this "mystery of iniquity" (2 Thess. 2:7, KJV), is irrevocably set against God's reign.

Jesus Reveals Sin

Knowledge of sin occurs in knowing Jesus Christ. As the definitive revelation of God, he is also the definitive revelation of sin. Throughout the Gospel of John, as the incarnate "I am," Jesus exposes spiritual darkness for all the disorder and the evil it breeds (John 1:5; 3:19; 8:12-35, 46; cf. Eph. 4:17-24). If he had not come to do the works of the Father, the world would not have known sin (John 15:25). Jesus knows what is in humankind (2:25). As the "light of the world" (8:12, NIV), Jesus shines in the darkness, and the darkness cannot overcome him (1:5; Gk., *katelaben* ["possess," "apprehend," "comprehend"]). Sin is darkness; Jesus is light (Gk., *phōs*). His work is that of the Father (5:30-32; 14:10-11) and the Holy Spirit (15:26-27; 16:5-11).

Jesus tells his disciples that when the Holy Spirit comes, he will "convince [Gk., *elenxei* ("convict," "rebuke," "reprove")] the world concerning sin and righteousness and judgment" (16:8). The Spirit will *convict* the world of sin and *convince* that Jesus is the revelation of the Father (vv. 12-15; cf. Luke 3:22; 1 Cor. 12:3; 1 John 5:6). The apostle Paul explains that the Father "searches the hearts of men" through the Holy Spirit (Rom. 8:27). Fleming Rutledge explains that

---

2. John Henry Newman, "General Answer to Mr. Kingsley," pt. 7 of *Apologia pro Vita Sua* (London: Longman, Green, Longman, Roberts, and Green, 1864), (orig. p. 335) 367, CCEL, http://www.ccel.org/ccel/newman/apologia.pdf.

God's prevenient grace, his advance mercy, reveals God's presence. His grace awakens awareness of sin by manifesting the distance between God's holiness and our sin. When this awakening happens, we are already in the circle of God's grace.[3]

Not the person who is lost, but the person who has been redeemed by Jesus Christ fully knows what it means to be a sinner. Fleming Rutledge refers to a sermon Karl Barth preached to prisoners on August 14, 1955, in his hometown of Basil, Switzerland. In this sermon, on Ephesians 2:8, Barth relates the following:

> You probably all know the legend of the rider who crossed the frozen Lake of Constance by night without knowing it. When he reached the opposite shore and was told whence he came, he broke down, horrified. This is the human situation when the sky opens and the earth is bright, when we may hear: *By grace you have been saved!* In such a moment we are like that terrified rider. When we hear this word we involuntarily look back, do we not, asking ourselves: Where have I been? Over an abyss, in mortal danger! What did I do? The most foolish thing I ever attempted! What happened? I was doomed and miraculously escaped and now I am safe![4]

Rutledge quotes Gary Anderson as commentary: "The notion of human sin and fallenness is nothing other than a considered reflection on the unmerited and unfathomable moment of salvation."[5] Rutledge explains that true knowledge of sin presupposes the prevenient activity of the Holy

---

3. Rutledge, *Crucifixion*, 174.

4. Karl Barth, *Deliverance to the Captives*, trans. M. Wieser (New York: Harper and Row, 1961), 38.

5. Gary A. Anderson, *Christian Doctrine and the Old Testament: Theology in the Service of Biblical Exegesis* (Grand Rapids: Baker Academic, 2017), 183.

Spirit. Apart from God's encircling mercy we would have no basis for understanding sin.[6]

First Major Error

When treating the meaning of sin, Christians often err by beginning with the sin of Adam and Eve. Then they proceed to the meaning of Jesus Christ. Adam and Eve, as fallen, are made to decide the purpose and meaning of Jesus. Adam and Eve do appear in the biblical narrative long before the birth of Jesus. However, they do not appear first when considering the meaning of sin. In the Christian faith, the biblical center and meaning of humankind's disobedience is disclosed by Jesus Christ, not Adam. Jesus is the full revelation of God, humanity, the meaning of sin, and reconciliation. Christians must think and speak from Christ the center.

Many habitually make Jesus only part of the biblical story instead of the interpretive center.

On the day of his resurrection, Christ completely reoriented the thinking of two disciples walking to Emmaus. He explained that from that day forward, he would be the interpretive center of all Scripture. The rest of the Bible is important, but it is only secondary and supportive. Testimony to Jesus is found "in all the Scriptures" (Luke 24:27, NIV), not in isolated proof texts. Richard B. Hays says, "The whole story of Israel builds to its narrative climax in Jesus. That is what Jesus tries to teach [the disciples] on the road. It is essential to teach them about Scripture because Scripture forms the matrix within which the recent shattering events in Jerusalem become intelligible."[7]

The writers of the New Testament absorbed Jesus's Emmaus tutorial. Paul, for example, knew the Father had

---

6. Rutledge, *Crucifixion*, 174.

7. Richard B. Hays, *Reading Backwards: Figural Christology and the Fourfold Gospel Witness* (2014; repr., Waco, TX: Baylor University Press, 2016), 14.

"set forth Christ as a plan for the fullness of time, to unite all things in him, things in heaven and things on earth" (Eph. 1:9-10; cf. 2 Cor. 1:19-22). New Testament writers had encountered and been transformed by the risen Lord. That explains why we call it the New Testament.

Jesus "endured [the] contradiction of sinners" (Heb. 12:3, KJV). In that endurance—his suffering on the cross— he revealed the nature of sin in all its hostility toward God. In his endurance, Christ is God's judgment against sin. With his "winnowing fork . . . in his hand" (Matt. 3:12, NIV), Jesus reveals the offence that makes atonement necessary. He forces sin into the open, strips it of all ambiguities and masks, and exposes its nakedness.[8]

Trying to understand or measure sin by criteria other than Jesus's revelation, or to judge sin by way of oneself or others, is "an inept and futile undertaking."[9] Knowledge of sin is not left to human judgment. Such efforts are void of the holy wrath of God and are consequently self-deceiving; sinners are not thrown back upon God's mercy. Self-analysis avoids confronting what Fleming Rutledge calls sin's cataclysmic disruption.[10]

Second Major Error

Christians err if they say the goal of salvation is to restore us to Adam before the fall.

Neither the Old nor the New Testaments teaches this. The goal of salvation is to transform Christians in the image of Christ, the new Adam (Rom. 5:12-17). He is the definitive Adam (v. 17); Christians are on a journey *in* and *toward* him, learning what it means to be human. By grace, through the Holy Spirit, the transformative vistas

---

8. Karl Barth, *Church Dogmatics*, vol. 4, *The Doctrine of Reconciliation*, pt. 1 (Edinburgh: T. and T. Clark International, 2004), 399.

9. Ibid., 403.

10. Rutledge, *Crucifixion*, 174.

of the new humanity are being explored. This process is sometimes called *theosis, Christification,* and sanctification. It means becoming more and more like God as revealed in Jesus Christ. The new creation is *in Christ Jesus* (Rom. 8:29; 2 Cor. 5:17; Eph. 4:22-24; Col. 1:21-22), not in retrieving the old creation.

In Romans, Paul explains how Christ undoes, overcomes, and moves beyond the first Adam (5:12-21). Grace reigns "through righteousness to eternal life through Jesus Christ our Lord" (v. 21). Paul Ricoeur observes that when the apostle Paul compares the first and second Adam in verses 12-21, he does so by means of a "similitude [which] brings to light a progression." When the apostle speaks of "how much more" (v. 17), he "excludes the possibility that the 'gift' should be a simple restoration of the order that prevailed before the 'fault'; the gift is the establishment of a new creation,"[11] new possibilities of love, forgiveness, creativity, community, and communion. The "old" is not the Christian faith's horizon. In this confidence, Christians are to confront impediments to the new creation.

Christian faith looks forward in hope to a new heaven and a new earth, to the consummation of God's kingdom (Gal. 5:5; Col 1:5, 27; Titus 1:2; Heb. 6:11-19), not backward in nostalgic yearning for an idyllic past.[12] "Then I saw a new heaven and a new earth; for the first heaven and the first earth had passed away, and the sea was no more" (Rev. 21:1).

Knowledge of Sin

Knowledge of sin is both a matter of revelation by the Holy Spirit (John 16:8-11) and faith, not a detached,

---

11. Ricoeur, *Symbolism of Evil*, 272.

12. Not once does Jeremiah mention Adam in his great anticipation of the new covenant (Jer. 31:31-34; 32:40). Adam is never mentioned by any of the prophets.

abstract topic to examine. We begin to know the nature of sin, including its despair (Rom. 3:9-20), when we have heard the gospel of Jesus Christ. Sin is manifested when we have become convinced by the Holy Spirit (John 16:8) that indeed Jesus is the Christ. It occurs when we have, by grace, obediently responded to the gift of faith that leads to reconciliation, to new birth through the Spirit, and to new creation in Christ Jesus.

Before we can receive the "good news" we must hear and believe the "bad news" that apart from God's mercy all humans are hopeless sinners (Rom. 3:21-26), judged so by God himself (vv. 21-26; 5:6-12). Pronouncing God's judgement upon sin is part of what Jesus said the Holy Spirit would do (John 16:8). The bad news must be owned through the convicting work of the Holy Spirit. Anyone who is not broken in response to hearing the gospel has probably not comprehended the word of God.[13] The Spirit tells us we are compliantly enslaved to a foreign power from which we cannot free ourselves. Make no mistake, the bad news is that we are idolatrous enemies of God. Minimize the bad news and the good is also minimized. Notice Paul's logic in 2 Corinthians 5:14: "For Christ's love compels us, because we are convinced that one died for all, and therefore all died" (NIV). It isn't that humans decide they have sinned and therefore need a Savior. Rather, the indictment is leveled against everyone by God's sovereign love, the love that provides a Redeemer for everyone *if* he or she will through obedient faith be "reconciled to God" (2 Cor. 5:20; cf. Eph. 2:1-10) through Christ, who bore sin's judgment for us (2 Cor. 5:21; 1 Pet. 3:18; 1 John 3:16).[14]

---

13. Rutledge, *Crucifixion*, 173.

14. God's gracious provision for salvation is *unconditional*. Clearly, its appropriation is *conditional*. No amount of rhetorical juggling by theologians can change this. "New creation" is offered to *all*.

Apart from revelation we may, says Robert W. Jenson, "speak meaningfully of fault and even of crime, but not of sin."[15] We have a true knowledge of sin when we are arrested by the Holy Spirit, when we can confess with Isaiah, "Woe is me! for I am undone!" (Isa. 6:5, KJV), or with the Philippian jailer, "What must I do to be saved?" (Acts 16:30, KJV). Opposition to God's judgment against us must be "beaten down once and for all." We "simply have to accept it and make it the starting point."[16]

Jenson stresses that this is particularly true of "religion" as humans create it. Religion, whatever its specific label, is a subtle and obstinate opponent of God's judgment. But when "the gospel occurs, it therefore confronts the human religious impulse whole and judges its hearers' religion by standards not provided by religion itself."[17] Even our concepts of God can become idolatrous unless they are persistently refined and corrected in practice by the Scriptures and orthodox Christian doctrine.

The "bad news" that precedes the "good news" is true self-knowledge. Kierkegaard said, "Every human existence, which is not transparently grounded in God . . . is after all despair."[18] The verdict passed against an awakened sinner by the Holy Spirit unmasks the "old man," the old self of sin, and exposes its truth before God. The old self must be crucified by Christ.

Sin as Unbelief and Idolatry

Sin manifests itself in external deeds. But the Bible first looks into the "depth of the heart with all its powers."[19]

---

15. Jenson, *Systematic Theology*, vol. 2, 133.

16. Barth, *Church Dogmatics*, vol. 4, *Doctrine of Reconciliation*, pt. 1, 398-99.

17. Jenson, *Systematic Theology*, vol. 2, 136.

18. Kierkegaard, "Sickness unto Death," 348.

19. Martin Luther, "Preface to the Epistle of St. Paul to the Romans," 1522, in *Martin Luther: Selections from His Writings*, ed. John Dillenberger (Garden City, NY: Doubleday, 1961), 22.

There, Martin Luther said, we discover "the root and the very source of all sin."[20] That source is *unbelief*, refusal to believe God—his promises, his law, his will for communion, and his provisions for human life. Unbelief exalts the flesh "and gives the desire to do works that are plainly wrong."[21] This was the sin of our first parents in the garden of Eden. "Christ therefore singled out unbelief and called it sin. In John, chapter 16:8, he says, 'The Spirit will convict the world of sin because they do not believe in me.'"[22]

Unbelief gives rise to idolatry (different in expression but not in essence). Idolatry elevates what is inescapably finite into the realm of deity. It slings its deadly consequences in all directions, including oppression of others (Isa. 5:8-10; Amos 4:1-5). It is "lust" as "sinful longing" (inordinate desire) broadly conceived. Injustice, the negation of true worship, is its deadly offspring. In Judah, idolatry sometimes descended into child sacrifice (2 Chron. 33:1-6; Jer. 7:31; Ezek. 20:26), even as "worship" in the temple continued! (Jer. 32:30-35; Ezek. 16:15-21). Idolatry is a brazen and persistent contradiction of the faithfulness and grace of God. Isaiah 2:8 comprehensively defines idolatry as bowing down to worship anything human fingers can fabricate. By it, humans "humiliate" (Hebr., *shapel*; Isa. 2:9; cf. Acts 7:39-42a) themselves. It always distorts what is essentially good—God's creation. Idolatry corrupts God-given powers in order to turn back and undermine God's purposes for humankind and the creation.[23] It boasts a power for itself—deity—it cannot sustain (1 Kings 18:20-29).

---

20. Ibid.

21. Ibid.

22. Ibid.

23. Wright, *Day the Revolution Began*, 308. For a jolting portrayal of the attraction and tenacity of idolatry, read Jeremiah's debate with the refugees in Egypt after the fall of Judah (Jer. 44:11-23).

But, says Robert Jenson, idolatry isn't confined to giving "divine honor to straightforwardly inappropriate objects." Rather, idolatry includes "our persistent and ingenious and even noble attempts to use deity for our own ends." Idols are whatever devices emerge.[24] "Service" to God or to one's neighbor, for example, can become but an instrument for promoting oneself or one's own religious affiliation.

Being finite by nature, idolatry must disfigure some part of God's creation for its survival. It brazenly distorts persons, families, nations, and cultures. Instead of reflecting God's wise order into the world, idolatry yields distortion, something grotesquely disfigured.[25]

Idolatry even set its sights on the incarnate Son of God: "Bow down" (Matt. 4:8, NIV; Mark 1:12-13; Luke 4:11-13). Richard Hays explains Satan's ultimate test was a temptation to idolatry (Matt. 4:8). Worship the power of "empire" the tempter intones. Use your divine authority to put the world aright through coercion, manipulation, and oppression. Crave and worship power as a sinful world defines it. Reward the cooperative, enslave the recalcitrant, and accept cringing adulation. In response, Jesus quotes Deuteronomy 6:13, which was "meant to secure Israel's exclusive covenantal relation to the one God." Jesus "declares his own allegiance to the one God of Israel and rejects worship of any other."[26] He embodies the covenant faithfulness Israel was supposed to render to God.[27]

Life According to the Flesh

Before good or bad deeds happen, unbelief, a refusal to trust and obey God, is present in the human heart. Un-

---

24. Jenson, *Systematic Theology*, vol. 2, 137.

25. Wright, *Day the Revolution Began*, 268.

26. Richard B. Hays, *Echoes of Scripture in the Gospels* (Waco, TX: Baylor University Press, 2016), 119.

27. Ibid., 120.

'Death and sin rule powerfully by pressing humans and technology into their service. Sin has carved out its own disruptive history, its own parasitic kingdom in God's good creation.

belief "exalts the flesh and brings [a] desire to do evil external works."[28] Exalting the flesh—what is inherently mortal and perishable, not *in itself* hostile toward God—means life "according to the flesh" (Rom. 8:5, 13; 7:5). Paul uses the Greek term *sarx* (flesh), *not sōma* (physical body). *Sarx* involves our entire creaturely existence, the inescapably fleshly character of human existence, not just our physical body. Life *"according* to *sarx"* as Paul means it, G. B. Caird explains, refers to "the whole sinful nature of unredeemed mankind. . . . To be 'in [or after, confidence in] the flesh' is the same thing as to be 'in Adam,' in the old humanity, enslaved to sin and death. Christians are not, in this sense, 'in the flesh' (Rom. 8:9)."[29] It is life lived at the level of decaying materiality; its fruit is always spiritual death.

When Paul says, "Wretched man that I am! Who will deliver me from this body of death?" (Rom. 7:24), he is speaking for the entire human race. He is echoing Jesus's charge that all of us have gone astray like lost sheep. This is our original fallenness, departure, a "body of death" from which we cannot free ourselves. All efforts to do so only confirm our sinful reliance "upon the flesh." Fleming Rutledge explains that the "body of death" encompasses the whole of human life ruled by the powers. It entails enslavement to sin, fear of being excluded by God, and terror at being judged and condemned.[30]

Sin as a Powerful, Ubiquitous Kingdom

Sin is "a power that lays hold of man." It is a "something," a "reality."[31] More than any other apostolic writer,

---

28. Luther, "Preface," 22.

29. G. B. Caird, *The Language and Imagery of the Bible* (Grand Rapids: Eerdmans, 1980). 44. According to Paul, "works of the flesh" include many that we should call sins of the spirit, such as envy and selfish ambition (Gal. 5:20) (44).

30. Rutledge, *Crucifixion*, 307.

31. Ricoeur, *Symbolism of Evil*, 70.

Paul makes *explicit* what is *implicit* in the Gospels (Rom. 5:12-19). Death and sin rule powerfully by pressing humans and technology into their service. Sin has carved out its own disruptive history, its own parasitic kingdom in God's good creation.

The New Testament knows sin is an active power or powers. In Romans, says N. T. Wright, Paul treats sin as a force. It is far more than a composite of sinful acts.[32] Sin results from idolatry, an act in which God-given powers are surrendered to malign forces. Slavery to sin results.[33] Jesus recognized his tempter as a power—Satan (Matt. 4:1; Mark 1:13; Luke 4:2). Scribes from Jerusalem accused Jesus of casting out demons by the power of Satan (Mark 3:22-27). Paul called Satan "the prince of the power of the air, the spirit that is now at work in the sons of disobedience" (Eph. 2:2). He told the Colossians they have been delivered "from the dominion [Gk., *exousias* ("domain," "jurisdiction")] of darkness" (Col. 1:13). Paul could even call iniquity a "mystery" (2 Thess. 2:7). On the cross Jesus "disarmed the principalities and powers and made a public example of them, triumphing over them in him" (Col. 2:15).

The kingdom of evil is ubiquitous—universal. Not only did humankind fall into bondage, but it also universally collaborates with and champions its power. According to Paul, says Fleming Rutledge, sin is a sinister power humans cannot control if left unaided.[34] True, sin is something people *do* (Rom. 3:23). But it is also a *dominion* under which humanity is enslaved (John 8:34; Rom. 3:9; 6:20). There is a kingdom of evil, a universal power that enlists humans in service to its cosmic goals.[35]

---

32. Wright, *Day the Revolution Began*, 280.
33. Ibid.
34. Rutledge, *Crucifixion*, 189.
35. Ibid., 435-36.

The Kingdom of Evil Converges

The kingdom of God has been inaugurated and is advancing toward its consummation. The kingdom of evil has been decisively judged by the *Alpha* and the *Omega*. The mystery of the gospel, hidden for ages, has been made known. The end of Satan's kingdom is sealed. And "through the church the manifold wisdom of God [is now being] made known to the principalities and powers in the heavenly places" (Eph. 3:10). But "the end is not yet" (Mark 13:7, ESV). The Son has not yet delivered the completed kingdom to the Father. Not all opponents of the kingdom have been "put . . . under his feet" (1 Cor. 15:24-25). The mopping-up campaign is yet to be completed. We may not fully understand all this, but recognizing the kingdom of evil's continued sinister, corporate, enslaving, and God-denying reality is essential for understanding sin and for understanding our assignment in the mission of God.

All four Gospels trace the constant buildup of hostility toward Jesus during his earthly ministry. It began with Herod's scheme to kill Jesus while an infant. Beginning with Jesus's early ministry, the Pharisees and the Herodians plotted against him. N. T. Wright says evil was steadily drawing itself up to its full height. In response, God was raising up his king to effect justice in God's creation.[36] Unbeknown to Satan, Jesus was making ready to bind "the strong man" and "plunder his house" (Mark 3:27). He would be "lifted up" (John 8:28; 12:32, NIV) and "glorified" (12:23; 13:31-32, NIV).

Finally, the powers of sin converged. In the events surrounding Jesus's crucifixion, evil is unleashed with one purpose: to destroy the Son of God. Then came the cross. Sin closed in for the kill. In Jesus's crucifixion the powers

---

36. Wright, *Day the Revolution Began*, 205.

of sin became incarnate. The deceitful nature of sin became unambiguous. The cross removes all lingering uncertainty about the nature of sin.

Conclusion

The kingdom of God has been decisively inaugurated; it has yet to be consummated. We live between the "already" and the "not yet" (see Phil. 1:6) in active and confident hope, not in uncertain, suspended animation. Jesus's kingdom parables have prepared us. "The kingdom of heaven is like a grain of mustard seed which a man took and sowed in his field" (Matt. 13:31). "The kingdom of heaven is like leaven which a woman took and hid in three measures of flour, till it was all leavened" (v. 33). Jesus taught what we should do in anticipation of the kingdom's consummation. "The kingdom of heaven is like a merchant in search of fine pearls, who, on finding one pearl of great value, went and sold all that he had and bought it" (vv. 45-46).

FOUR

Sin
The Sickness unto Death (Part 2)

In this chapter we begin with the three expressions of sin. Then we consider (1) how the Old Testament understands sin, (2) how the New Testament understands sin, and (3) sin against the creation. Recall the words of Paul Ricoeur: "The Bible never speaks of sin except in the perspective of the salvation that delivers from sin. The 'pedagogy' of the human race makes the pessimism of the fall abound in order that the optimism of salvation may superabound" (John 1:14-16; Rom. 5:20).[1]

Three Expressions of Sin[2]

Knowledge of sin, through knowledge of Jesus Christ, yields knowledge of (1) rebellion against God, (2) enmity with one's neighbor, and (3) sin against oneself. These may not be seen equally in each person. "Not every man who denies God openly hates his fellow, nor does everyone who hates his fellow man openly deny God, nor is it necessarily apparent that either the one or the other is engaged in self-destruction; and there are many who are obviously de-

---

1. Ricoeur, *Symbolism of Evil*, 264.
2. Barth speaks of "the three moments of evil." For the sake of clarity I have restated the three as the "three expressions of sin." Barth, *Church Dogmatics*, vol. 4, *Doctrine of Reconciliation*, pt. 1, 398.

stroying themselves without appearing either to deny God or to hate their fellows, let alone both."[3]

Equality of expression is not the point. The point is inseparability. From the universal and true divine judgment that "all have sinned and fall short of the glory of God" (Rom. 3:23; 11:32), the *second* and *third* expressions follow. Failure to love God in obedient worship makes it impossible to love what God loves—one's neighbor and oneself in community. Disruption in the first order leads to disruption and distortion in the other two. Unhinged from obedient love for God, we no longer know who the neighbor or the self is, or how to love either one. Rebellion disfigures every dimension of human life. It unleashes exploitation and/or idolatry in every direction, resulting in fragmentation and estrangement where wholeness and community were intended. Creation as divinely ordered life ceases. How could it be otherwise? Apart from him in whom the life of God is manifest and given, there is no life (John 1:4; 3:16, 36; 5:24; 6:35).

The Gospel of John makes this crystal clear. "Truly, truly, I say to you, unless you eat the flesh of the Son of man and drink his blood, you have no life in you; he who eats my flesh and drinks my blood has eternal life, and I will raise him up at the last day" (6:53-54).

Part of the folly and lie of sin is that the second and third expressions of sin can be avoided even if one is guilty of the first; supposedly loving God is unnecessary for correctly knowing and loving one's neighbor and oneself. But Jesus said, "Whoever believes in the Son has eternal life, but whoever rejects the Son will not see life, for God's wrath remains on them" (3:36, NIV). Spiritual death spreads into all horizontal relationships. Jesus is the author and head of the new and true humanity. Apart from Christ, love for one's neighbor and oneself miscarries.

---

3. Ibid.

By contrast, a major characteristic of the modern era is belief that by correctly using human reason and effort, society can be successfully organized without reference to Christ. We now live in a "brave new world" in which "man has come of age." Belief in God, Friedrich Nietzsche said, had been humankind's greatest retardant. Now that God lies "in the grave," "higher men" can arise. "Now only cometh the great noontide, now only doth the higher man become—master!"[4]

On the other hand, one cannot love God without loving one's neighbor as oneself. The two parts of the Great Commandment are inseparable (Matt. 22:36-40; Mark 12:30-31; John 13:31-35). "If any one says, 'I love God,' and hates his brother, he is a liar; for he who does not love his brother whom he has seen, cannot love God whom he has not seen. And this commandment we have from him, that he who loves God should love his brother also" (1 John 4:20-21).

Sin's three expressions first appeared in the garden of Eden. They have plagued human life ever since. Augustine cataloged the failures of "the city of man" in his *City of God*. The earthly city attempts to establish itself apart from God. Its failure is marked by the fact that "this city is often divided against itself by litigations, wars, quarrels, and such victories as are either life-destroying or short-lived."[5]

---

4. Friedrich Nietzsche, "The Higher Man," ch. 73 in pt. 4 of *Thus Spake Zarathustra*, 1883, trans. Thomas Common (New York: Macmillan, 1916; repr., Project Gutenberg, 2008), https://www.gutenberg.org/files/1998/1998-h/1998-h.htm#link2H_4_0052.

5. Augustine, *The City of God*, bk. 15, ch. 4, in vol. 2 of *Nicene and Post-Nicene Fathers* (series I), ed. Philip Schaff (reprint of 1886 edition), CCEL, https://www.ccel.org/ccel/schaff/npnf102.pdf.

A "Map" of Sin

The three expressions discussed above (rebellion against God, enmity with one's neighbor, and sin against oneself) provide a "map" of sin as viewed in the Old and New Testaments. The Bible chronicles how the second and third quickly followed the first and spread like aggressive cancer through the human race.

Immediately after disobeying God in the garden, communal as well as personal consequences followed. Genesis reveals sin's individual character. It also reveals sin as transmitted corporately—in social structures—from one generation to another. Adam and Eve turned against each other. Cain murdered his brother, Abel, and subsequently bore "punishment . . . greater than I can bear" (Gen. 4:13). The "wickedness of man was great in the earth, and . . . every imagination of the thoughts of his heart was only evil continually" (6:5; cf. Rom. 5:12-14; 1 Cor. 15:22).

The flood, recorded in Genesis 7–8, did not cleanse the earth of sin. In Genesis 11, God confuses the language of presumptuous city dwellers who fancy themselves able to reach the heavens. God destroys two corrupt cities, Sodom and Gomorrah, because of their appalling wickedness (19:1-38). Jacob, with his mother's help, deceives Isaac his father and Esau his brother, cheating Esau out of his father's rightful blessing (27:1-36).

There is more: Israel worshipping the golden calf and thereby breaking Israel's covenant with God (Exod. 32:1-10), the beginning of Israel's idolatry after settling in Canaan (Ezek. 20:27-28), gross corruption of the priesthood by Eli's sons (1 Sam. 2:12-36), and David's adultery with Bathsheba and his murder of Uriah (2 Sam. 11:1-27). The list can be extended.

The prophets recognized and exposed the corporate and individual character of sin. Facing impending destruction by Assyria, and having forsaken obedient worship of

Yahweh, Israel, the Northern Kingdom, was selling "the righteous for silver, and the needy for a pair of shoes"; the powerful were trampling "the head of the poor into the dust" and ignoring the needs "of the afflicted" (Amos 2:6-7). Amos verbally lacerates affluent women of Samaria who were sucking luxurious juices from a social system unjustly built on the backs of the poor. Two hundred years later, Jeremiah prophesied to Judah amid its advanced disease of idolatry. Judah's priests were handling "the law" but knew nothing of Yahweh. Prophets were prophesying "by Ba'al." The populace had forsaken "the fountain of living waters" (Jer. 2:8-13).

As they catalog the sins of Israel and Judah, Amos, Isaiah, Jeremiah, and the other prophets expose sin as personal, corporate, and institutional. Religious and social structures God intended as vehicles for promoting worship, justice, and human flourishing have been harnessed in sin's employment. The temple, the home, the courts, government, agriculture, and the economy have all become sin's clients and entrepreneurs. Perverted structures enflame personal evil; personal evil stokes the fires of structural evil.

If we fail to recognize the structural character of sin, evil is only partially understood and exposed. Forms of Christianity that do not come to terms with structured evil do a disservice to Scripture, to their communicants, to the complexity of human life, to grace, and to the hope of new creation.

How the Old Testament Understands Sin

Walter Brueggemann says Old Testament faith has a "broad and deep notion of sin commensurate with its all-pervading conviction about God."[6] Knowledge of sin comes through knowledge of God. "God, who creates,

---

6. Brueggemann, *Reverberations of Faith*, 195.

governs, and wills a world of well-being with and for all of God's creatures, forms the context for sin; sin is the violation of God's will for [the] . . . well-being willed by the creator God."[7]

The Old Testament focuses on three terms: (1) sin as deficit, failure, or mistake (*hatta't*); (2) sin as recalcitrance and rebellion (*pesha'*); and (3) sin as moral violation (*'awon*). Although each term has a different root, for practical purposes they can be treated as synonymous (Exod. 34:7).

Relying upon Brueggemann, we examine sin in the Old Testament from three perspectives: (1) sin as God centered, (2) life as ordered by Torah, and (3) sin as an intruder.

Sin as God Centered

Humans are created by God and for God. They are meant to live in "glad, obedient responsiveness to God."[8] Sin involves a "distortion or violation" of God's ordering of creation; humans refuse to be dependent and responsive. "The distortion and violation of creatureliness is fundamentally a distortion of relationship with God—a refusal to be in a relationship of glad praise, thanks, and obedience."[9]

Sin is understood within the context of covenant. God is unfailingly faithful, and Israel is expected to be also. "The basis of a covenantal existence with God is the premise that obedient living leads to well-being and disobedience leads to trouble and death (Deut. 30:15-20)."[10] This is the assumption of a covenantal ethic.[11]

God keeps sin from becoming the defining reality of his creation. "God's capacity to deal effectively with sin is a

---

7. Ibid, 195. In *Sin: A History* (New Haven, CT: Yale University Press, 2010), Gary A. Anderson shows that in the Old Testament especially, sin has a history, as revealed in the changing metaphors and language used to identify sin (4-6).

8. Brueggemann, *Reverberations of Faith*, 196.

9. Ibid.

10. Ibid.

11. Ibid.

Sin rejects coherence between true worship of God, moral wholeness, and love for one's neighbor as commanded in the Decalogue. One cannot love God apart from loving one's neighbor.

celebrated certitude in the Old Testament." By a sovereign act, God is willing and able to pardon and forgive sins (Jer. 31:34) when they are acknowledged and confessed (Ps. 51:1-10). God has generously provided the means whereby "the worship procedures of Israel give concrete, available, institutional ways for forgiveness and rehabilitation" (Lev. 1–7).[12]

God forgives and brings scattered exiles home. "The Sovereign LORD says: I will gather you from the nations and bring you back from the countries where you have been scattered. . . . I will remove from them their heart of stone and give them a heart of flesh" (Ezek. 11:17-19, NIV).

Life as Ordered by Torah

Torah means "instruction." Proper relationship between God and his creation is ordered and guided by the commands of Torah, the Law, as summarized in the Decalogue—the Ten Commandments. Bernhard Anderson explains the Torah is "divine guidance or direction which God gives his people in their historical pilgrimage."[13] Violation of Torah, of worshipful relationship with God, yields disorder, disruption, judgment, guilt, and death.

Broadly, Torah has two foci. *First*, a right "relationship with the creator God evokes a concern for holiness (purity, cleanness) . . . (Lev. 19:2)." *Second*, worship of God must be expressed in "the practice of societal justice in political and economic terms, so that 'love of God' inescapably mandates concern for the neighbor, particularly for the disadvantaged or needy neighbor (see Prov. 17:5; Mark 12:28-31)."[14] "Hate evil, and love good, and establish justice in the gate" (Amos 5:15). Sin rejects coherence between true worship of God, moral wholeness, and love for one's neighbor as command-

---

12. Ibid., 197.
13. Anderson, *Understanding the Old Testament*, 10.
14. Brueggemann, *Reverberations of Faith*, 196.

ed in the Decalogue. One cannot love God apart from loving one's neighbor.[15]

Brueggemann notes that by and large the consequences of disobeying Torah "are produced in the very process of violation." Consequently, they do not ordinarily involve God's wrath. "The act of the wayward creature tends to issue its own sanction."[16]

Sin as an Intruder

The Old Testament treats sin as an intruder. It is "neither the defining mark of human personality nor the defining characteristic of life with God."[17] "Creatureliness may have within it the seeds of sin, but the Old Testament is clear that sin is not an inescapable product of creatureliness."[18] Sin does not *belong*. The creation, including humans, is *essentially* good. Six times during the creative process God observes that what he has made is "good" (Gen. 1:4, 10, 12, 18, 21, 25). After humans have been created, God recaps his work by observing that it is "very good" (1:31). The creation is "good" by virtue of its origin—the good God.

Old Testament scholar Alex Varughese says that in order to be true to the biblical text we must recognize elements of disorder or chaos were present in the creation from the beginning.[19] God's speeches in the book of Job (chs. 38–41) clearly imply order and disorder are part of God's design for creation. For example, Job pictures Behemoth and Leviathan (chs. 40–41) as monstrous and disorderly creatures set within divinely established bound-

---

15. Ibid.
16. Ibid.
17. Ibid.
18. Ibid.
19. Alex Varughese, telephone conversation with author, November 28, 2018.

aries; though fearsome to humans, they live in fear of, and submission to, the power of their maker.

The biblical accounts of creation, says New Testament scholar G. B. Caird, constitute a "declaration of faith that the world originated in a victory of order over chaos, a summons to the worshipper to enlist with the army of light in the ongoing battle against the forces of darkness, a confident assertion of the ultimate victory of good over evil."[20]

Well-intended people often say, "Humans are essentially evil." Nothing could be farther from the truth. The "essence" of anything is "that without which it could not be." A tree *essentially* absorbs carbon monoxide, not oxygen. A baby cries *essentially*. If it did not, something would be wrong. If humans were *essentially* evil, hoping for their redemption would amount to hoping they might become something other than human. Humans are fallen. But that isn't their essence. Their essence is the image of God. Hence, that image can be restored.

The Old Testament never denies the presence of evil in God's creation. But evil is always present as disobedience and as a distortion of what God created as "good." In spite of its kingdom-like quality and aggressive opposition to God's reign, evil has no independent metaphysical status, no independent source of being. Evil is a parasite or cancer in God's good creation, deriving all its "life" from what it distorts. Darkness is the absence of light. To exist, evil must deprecate what belongs to God alone. This does not explain the "ultimate" origin of evil. But it does explain its "nature."

We should carefully avoid speaking of the creation, the natural order, as itself fallen or sinful. Humans sin; the creation does not. The creation can be unwillingly and almost infinitely pressed into sin's hire. But when that happens,

---

20. Caird, *Language and Imagery of the Bible*, 226.

the creation becomes sin's slave, not its willing ally. The tree carved into an idol is forced into that form (Isa. 44:12-17).

Christians sound foolish when they speak of a fallen creation, as though sin has somehow affected the principles by which the universe functions. Photosynthesis (the complex process by which carbon dioxide is converted into green plants) is not the result of sin. But humans can sinfully abuse God's intended ecological system in ways that yield evil. Earthquakes result from tectonic-plate shifts, not from an "evil" earth. "Mountains and all hills, fruit trees and all cedars! Beasts and all cattle, creeping things and flying birds! . . . Praise the LORD!" (Ps. 148:9-10, 14, RSV). Walter Brueggemann notes that in the Old Testament Wisdom Literature, "'foolishness' is a term used for failure to respect the . . . nonnegotiable ordering of creation."[21]

Astonishingly, as abominable as sin is, and as violently as it assails God, the neighbor, oneself, and community, God does not give up on his world. The Old and New Testaments declare the steadfast love of the God of all grace (Ps. 111:4; Eph. 1:7).

How the New Testament Understands Sin

In this section, key Greek words must be considered.

The angel told Joseph that Mary's son, Jesus Messiah, would "save his people from their sins" (Matt. 1:21, NIV). While John the Baptist was baptizing people in the Jordan River, he saw Jesus coming toward him. John exclaimed, "Behold, the Lamb of God, who takes away the sin of the world" (John 1:29). The apostle Paul says, "For our sake [God] made [Christ] to be sin who knew no sin, so that in him we might become the righteousness of God" (2 Cor. 5:21). In Christ, on the cross, God has reconciled "the world to himself" (2 Cor. 5:19).

---

21. Brueggemann, *Reverberations of Faith*, 195-96.

What crisis could have been so grave as to lead the eternal God of holy love to do all this? The answer is sin. In harmony with the Old Testament, the New Testament exposes sin in a way that can only be comprehended in the light of the cross. There God Incarnate took upon himself the sin of the world and made atonement for all humankind. In the New Testament, the full power of sin is revealed only as one comes to know Christ.

Uniformly, the New Testament testifies that because of sin and apart from the cross, we are "helplessly trapped inside [our] own worst self, miserably aware of the chasm between the way we are and the way God intends us to be" (see Rom. 6:18; Eph. 2:1).[22]

The apostle Paul insists individual sins proceed from a universal sinful condition. Sin is a "racial" (the human race) problem. God's judgement against sin includes all people. All humans are "in" Adam; "one man's trespass led to condemnation for all men" (5:18). Fallen, all humans have in themselves confirmed Adam's rebellion. There is a solidarity of disobedience, idolatry, and justifiable "condemnation for all men" (v. 18). In Romans 5:12-21, Paul gives all humankind the name "Adam," a judgment owned by each person as the Holy Spirit searches hearts and compels honesty: "In Adam all die" (1 Cor. 15:22). "Sin came into the world through one man and death through sin, and so death spread to all men because all men sinned" (Rom. 5:12). Sin is God's enemy. Its end, or "fruit," is death (see 5:21; 6:23; 7:5; 8:6).

It is not sufficient to admit we are all "in Adam" and in bondage to sin. Though slaves, we each have become complicit in our slavery; we have become eager agents of sin.[23]

---

22. Ibid., 174.
23. Ibid, 179.

To glimpse the sin that Christ became (2 Cor. 5:21) and "bore" (1 Pet. 2:24), let's examine the major terms the New Testament uses for sin.

The terms most often used are *hamartia* and *adikia*.[24]

Hamartia

Hamartia is the word from which we derive the word "hamartiology," the doctrine of sin. *Hamartia* means "missing the mark." The Hebrew equivalent is *hatta't*. But this does not mean we have aimed at the correct target and missed, but as sinners, we have aimed at the wrong mark and hit it dead center. We have done this corporately and personally, institutionally and individually; one feeds the other. Human structures and individuals justify the indictment. God's grace takes sin's measure, both in exposing it and in new creation. The "inventiveness" of evil for sinning against God, one's neighbor, and oneself constitutes the "mystery of iniquity" (2 Thess. 2:7, KJV; Gk., *anomias* ["of lawlessness," "of wickedness," "of unrighteousness"]). (Structural evil is the topic of ch. 8.)

Hamartia is the comprehensive expression for everything opposed to God. All other concepts and synonyms are overshadowed by *hamartia* and are to be understood in its light. Along with its cognates, *hamartia* refers to offenses against morals, laws, people, and gods.

Hamartia refers to humankind's sin, which is always directed against God. The verb form means "to miss the mark" or "to sin." The noun form means a "sin," a "transgression," or a "sinner." The adjective form means "sinful." *Hamartia* is used 173 times, 64 of which are used by Paul. He uses *hamartia* 48 times in Romans alone. *Hamartēma*, a "sin," a "transgression," is used five times and refers to

---

24. My examination of the New Testament terms relies on Colin Brown, ed., *The New International Dictionary of New Testament Theology*, vol. 3 (Grand Rapids: Zondervan, 1979), 573-85.

an individual act (1 Cor. 6:18). It is used in the context of forgiveness in Mark 3:28 and Romans 3:25.

Paul most often uses *hamartia* in the singular. Sin is treated almost as a personal power that acts in and through humans (Rom. 5:12, 21; 6:6, 17; 7:9-11). The same is true of *sarx* ("flesh"; see Gal. 5:19, 24) and *thanatos* ("death"; see Rom. 6:9*b*). "Paul's statements on the universality of sin since Adam (Rom. 5) [contributed] to the church's doctrine of original sin."[25] Fleming Rutledge explains that we should not think of sin as a composite of individual misdeeds. Rather, it is a malevolent cosmic power whose goal is to corrupt God's creation, to imprison and visit death upon it. Militantly, sin aims at disrupting God's purposes. Individual sins reveal this malevolent agency as universally operative. Sin is God's cosmic enemy as well as ours.[26]

In the Johannine literature, *hamartia* is used in the context of the incarnation, which holds together heaven and earth. Jesus, who is without sin, comes into the world and, as the Lamb of God, sheds his precious blood for the sin of the world (John 1:29; 1 John 3:5).

Adikia

Adikia (Hebr. equivalent, *'awon*) is less specific and more varied than *hamartia*. It describes the outwardly visible characteristics of what stands under the power of sin. James 3:6 is an example; injustice is perpetuated by the tongue. Similarly, Luke 16:1-9 refers to unjust mammon. In Romans 1:18-32, when Paul describes the sins of the Gentiles, he uses *adikia* and *asebeia* ("wickedness," "godlessness," "impiety"), not *hamartia*.

---

25. Ibid., 581.
26. Rutledge, *Crucifixion*, 175.

Adikia comes from the legal arena. It is the opposite of righteousness (*dikaiosynē*).[27] It connotes unrighteousness, dealing unjustly, unjust deeds, wrong doing, and to injure. It can mean behavior that does not conform to the moral norm (Matt. 5:45; Luke 18:11; John 7:18; 2 Thess. 2:12). *Adikia* mostly occurs in the singular, which indicates its attention is upon the whole phenomenon of transgression, not just upon individual acts of sin. In ancient Israel it meant offense against the sacral order of divine justice. *Adikia* affects and can destroy community. God demands covenant people to purge evil from their midst (Lev. 16:21).

The verb form, *adikeō*, is used twenty-five times in the New Testament, where it means "to act unjustly," "to do harm in relation to others" (Matt. 20:13; Acts 7:24, 26-27; Gal. 4:12). It is always found in relationships between humans (Acts 7:24; 1 Cor. 6:7; 2 Cor. 7:12). Paul and John contrast *adikia* with *alētheia* (truth) (John 7:18; Rom. 1:18; 2:8). Second Timothy 2:19 warns unrighteousness is not compatible with calling on God's name. Peter emphasizes the final judgment and God's condemnation of the *adikoi* (2 Pet. 2:9, 13, 15).

New Testament scholar Michael J. Gorman says that according to Romans 1 it is clear that *adikia*, injustice, is the primary, categorical expression of sin. For its resolution it must be addressed at its root, not simply by forgiving diverse manifestations. In Romans 12:1-2, "transformation, not merely forgiveness, marks the justified community," where the undoing of Romans 1 is manifested.[28]

---

27. N. T. Wright says *dikaiosynē* should be translated "faithfulness to the covenant," not as God's moral status or achievements. Wright, *Day the Revolution Began*, 81-82.

28. Gorman, *Inhabiting the Cruciform God*, 95.

Akatharsia

Akatharsia means "impurity," "uncleanness." It is used repeatedly in the Pauline Epistles to name a pattern of life enslaved to sin. "Therefore God gave them up in the lusts of their hearts to impurity" (Rom. 1:24*a*). As slaves to sin, the Roman Christians "once yielded [their] members to impurity [*akatharsia*] and to greater and greater iniquity [*anomia* ("lawlessness," "iniquity," "wickedness")]" (6:19). "Darkened in their understanding, alienated from the life of God," the Gentiles "have given themselves up . . . to practice every kind of uncleanness" (*akatharsia*; Eph. 4:18-19). Paul exhorts the Colossian Christians to "put to death . . . fornication, impurity [*akatharsia*], passion, evil desire, and covetousness, which is idolatry" (Col. 3:5; cf. 2 Cor. 12:21; Gal. 5:19; Eph. 5:3; 1 Thess. 2:3; 4:7). *Akatharsia* is a polluting force that can spread and harmfully impact communities.

Parabasis

Parabasis is a synonym for *adikia*. *Parabasis* and its cognates refer to a transgression of the law. They throw light on *adikia*.

Paraptōma

Paraptōma, which comes from *parapiptō*, means a "false step," "falling down beside," "losing one's way," "erring," and "trespassing." Generally it means a "moral lapse and willful offense."

Additional Concepts

Additional concepts that belong to the wider concept of sin are (1) *anomia*: "lawlessness" (*nomos* [law]); (2) *asebeia*: "godlessness"; (3) *ptaiō*: "stumble," "come to grief"; (4) *hēttēma*: "defeat"; (5) *hysterēma*: "lack," "fault"; (6) *planaō*: "go astray," "deceive oneself"; (7) *agnoeō*: "not know," "not understand"; (8) *opheilō*: "be under obligation"; and (9) *parakoē*: "disobedience." Three terms are associated with guilt: (1) *aitia*: "cause," "accusation"; (2) *elenchō*: "convict"; and (3) *enochos*: "guilty."

In summary, in the New Testament, the criterion for unrighteousness is the righteousness of God (Rom. 3:5, 26; 9:14), which reveals unrighteousness (3:5). The chasm opened by unrighteousness can be bridged only by Christ, the Righteous One, who stands in our place (3:24; 2 Cor. 5:21; 1 Pet. 3:18).

Sin against the Creation

Discussion of sin is incomplete unless it includes sin against God's creation. God's relationship with his creation, as the Bible consistently celebrates, establishes its abuse as a matter of grave theological importance. If the creation were inherently evil, as ancient Gnostics taught, abusing it would have no religious or moral significance. But the Bible declares that not only is God the Creator, but he also continues to sustain and care for his world (Col. 1:15-17; Heb. 1:3) and intends its complete redemption (Isa. 65:17; Rom. 8:18-25; Rev. 21:1-4). Every species, no matter how humble, comments entomologist E. O. Wilson, "is a masterpiece of biology, and well worth saving."[29]

Old Testament scholar John H. Walton shows that the creation account in Genesis 1 focuses on the generation of a cosmic temple with all its functions, and with God dwelling in it.[30] "God is," adds William P. Brown, "the consummate royal priest"[31] who designates humans as his "authorized agents and representatives in the world."[32] In

---

29. E. O. Wilson, *The Creation: An Appeal to Save Life on Earth* (New York: W. W. Norton and Company, 2006), 5.

30. John H. Walton, *The Lost World of Genesis One: Ancient Cosmology and the Origins Debate* (Downers Grove, IL: IVP Academic, 2009), 78-86.

31. William P. Brown, *The Seven Pillars of Creation: The Bible, Science, and the Ecology of Wonder* (Oxford, UK: Oxford University Press, 2010), 46.

32. Ibid., 48.

Isaiah 6:3, the angel declares, "The whole earth is full of [God's] glory." Psalm 148:1-5 exhorts a cosmic choir to burst forth in praise and worship. God's creation is properly sacred, but not divine.

The New Testament is as confident that God is the Creator as is the Old Testament. The Gospel of John opens with the same words the Greek version of Genesis uses (*en archē* [in the beginning]) to begin the story of creation. In Revelation, an angel swears "by him who lives for ever and ever, who created heaven and what is in it, the earth and what is in it" (Rev. 10:6). The apostle Paul declares God created "all things by Jesus Christ" (Eph. 3:9, KJV). In Colossians he adds that not only were all things in heaven and earth created "through him and for him," but also "in him all things hold together" (Col. 1:16-17; *synistēmi* ["constitute," "bring or band together"]). John Walton says the Bible supports the view that as Creator, God "continues to sustain the [creation's] functions moment by moment."

The book of Revelation declares this same Christ will transform the creation into new creation (Rev. 21:1-8). In astonishing language consistent with his Hebrew faith, the apostle Paul numbers the creation among the children of God. Against its will, the creation has been subjected to futility. It now waits "with eager longing" (Rom. 8:19) for the consummation of God's kingdom, when it will be delivered from slavery to corruption. It *knows* it will be included in the glories of kingdom consummation (vv. 18-25), the final and universal *shalom* ("peace" [Gk., *eirēnē*]) of God (Rev. 21:1-6).

Therefore, it is necessary to say that creation care is not only a biblical topic but also a christological and kingdom mandate. Disregard for God's creation is sinful. Treating God's cosmic temple as less than a christological issue departs from the New Testament and perilously slides in the direction of Gnostic dualism. Given what the Bible teaches about God and his creation, it is amazing that we can so often speak of salvation while hardly mentioning the creation. Neither the Old nor the New Testaments support a narrow anthropocentrism. Just as there is no humanity apart from the creation (Gen. 2:7), even so there is no salvation that excludes God's creation (Rom. 8:18-25); Creator and Redeemer are inseparable (Col. 1:15-20).

Humans have always been able to abuse God's creation in some way. Idolatry in the ancient world was a form of sinning against creation; it forced parts of God's creation into service against him. The consequences were largely visited upon the abusers. The arrival of technology and industrialization in the modern era changed things dramatically. Technology required vast changes in how raw materials, such as coal used for firing blast furnaces, were extracted and used. Many times the natural world has been exploited with little or no consideration for its impact upon humans and animal life.

Today, ideological biases inserted into debates about climate change make it difficult to distinguish fact from fiction, reputable science from junk science. But Christians need not resolve all the debates about ecology to take stock of how we humans have polluted and disfigured God's cosmic temple by behaving more like selfish autonomous owners than appointed stewards. We must ask, In what condition are we transferring our stewardship to our children?

Love for God and for his cosmic temple requires (1) recognition of the kingdom importance of creation, (2) recognition that our narrow anthropocentric view of salvation that minimizes stewardship for God's cosmic temple is indefensible, (3) individual and corporate recognition of our sins of abuse, (4) confession, (5) an individual determination to remediate the abuses in all ways practical, (6) a determination to engage in corporate and global remediation in all ways possible, and (7) anticipation of renewed creation—this creation—as central to Easter faith (Eph. 1:10).[33]

Conclusion

How we treat God's cosmic temple says much about what we really believe about the incarnation and salvation. First John combated early forms of Gnosticism that denied Jesus's full humanity. Satisfying the Gnostic interests in salvation did not require a real physical Jesus.

John strongly disagreed. "I have seen him with my own eyes. I have touched him with hands. I know Jesus was fully human" (1 John 1:1, author paraphrase). Why was John so insistent? First, it was true. Second, the whole creation owes its existence to God. John knew that God intends to leave nothing of his creation abandoned. And he knew that if God were to shun becoming human—the incarnation—none of the rest of creation could be redeemed. Anything less would have been a divine failure.

Creation care, therefore, is an affirmation of the incarnation, an affirmation of the gospel, and an affirmation that the New Temple named Jesus has made the Father and his plans known, "full of grace and truth" (John 1:14, 18). Such convictions, says N. T. Wright, entail that creation care be considered an integral part of the church's mission, for it is integral to the mission of God.[34]

---

33. See N. T. Wright's explanation of the relationship between Jesus as Sabbath fulfillment and New Creation in "Discerning the Dawn: Knowing God in the New Creation," YouTube Video, 1:12:15, posted by "fleetwd1," May 8, 2017, https://www.youtube.com/watch?v=ZGX4EcJFupQ.

34. Wright, *Paul: A Biography* (San Francisco: HarperOne, 2018), 414-15.

Without One Plea
Grace That Takes the Measure of Life

FIVE

Ruby Turpin, the hog farmer, "a respectable, hard-working, church-going woman,"[1] didn't need God's grace. She knew who she was. But she could identify all the people who did need God's grace and her pity.[2] They included everyone lower than she on the social ladder, including poor people she considered common white trash. At night, while Claud, her husband, slept, Ruby would identity all the social classes. She placed those who owned land above ordinary people. She and Claud were landowners. Above them were people with a lot of money and much bigger houses and much more land. But before long the complexity of it all would overwhelm Ruby because some people with a lot of money were actually ordinary people and ought to be classed beneath her and Claud. There were even blacks who owned land. Usually, by the time Ruby fell asleep, she had lost track of her classifications.[3]

Mrs. Turpin's habit of classifying people according to their social location reached an abrupt crisis in a crowded doctor's waiting room. She and Claud were there because a

---

1. Flannery O'Connor, "Revelation," in *Flannery O'Connor: The Complete Stories* (New York: Farrar, Straus and Giroux, 1971), 502.

2. Ibid., 492.

3. Ibid., 491-92.

cow had kicked Claud in the head. Upon entering the waiting room, Mrs. Turpin immediately began sizing up everyone. There was a "lean stringy old fellow," a "well-dressed gray-haired lady" and a five- or six-year-old child who had a runny nose. He was dressed in a dirty blue playsuit.[4]

There were also a woman and her daughter—an ugly college student who also acted ugly. Her name was Mary Grace. Her eyes blazed. Mary Grace stared at Mrs. Turpin as if she had always known and resented her.[5] While Mrs. Turpin was praising Jesus for making her who she was and nobody else, Mary Grace hurled a book that struck Ruby in her left eye. Before Ruby could say anything, the girl crashed across the table and howled at Ruby. The girl's eyes focused on Mrs. Turpin and now seemed much brighter. It was as if a door tightly closed behind her eyes had opened.[6] As Mrs. Turpin looked into the girl's brilliant eyes, they locked on Ruby's eyes. Mary Grace whispered, "Go back to hell where you came from, you old wart hog." The girl's words struck Mrs. Turpin with full force.[7] There was no doubt the girl knew Ruby perfectly well.[8] Any effort to deny the girl's judgment would have been pointless.[9] God's strange grace had found Ruby Turpin and revealed the truth about her.

Arrested by God's Grace

Ruby Turpin had been arrested by the grace of God and marched off captive by the Holy Spirit. Grace had *prevened* through an ugly girl named Grace. Amazing grace? Amazing God! There was much work left to do. But the

4. Ibid., 488.
5. Ibid., 492, 495, 498.
6. Ibid., 499-500.
7. Ibid., 500.
8. Ibid.
9. Ibid., 502.

grace that "goes before" recognition of sin, that *precedes* confession, repentance, and forsaking sin, had pointedly arrived in the form of a hurled book.

But who is this self-righteous Ruby Turpin? Who is this woman who could boast that there are no common persons around—black or white—that she hasn't helped. Every day she works herself to the bone, not to mention all she does for the church.[10]

She is Saul of Tarsus, confident of his righteousness before God, on his way to Damascus with authority from the high priest, "breathing threats and murder against the disciples of the Lord," when "suddenly a light from heaven flashed about him. And he fell to the ground and heard a voice saying to him, 'Saul, Saul, why do you persecute me?'" (Acts 9:1-4).

Who is Ruby Turpin? She is each person who has arranged all the classes of people by their value and by what they deserve, who has located himself or herself in the social structure and is certain he or she doesn't need a "revelation" of his or her own sinfulness. She is every person who is arrested by the Holy Spirit, convicted of his or her sins, stripped of his or her self-righteousness and self-sufficiency, and hauled into the presence of the God of all grace. And she is every Christian who believes his or her accumulated holiness can now replace radical dependence upon God's grace. Like Mrs. Turpin, such Christians can show God they are "respectable, hard-working, and church-going." Mrs. Turpin was scandalized by God for singling her out through Mary Grace. He had overlooked a woman in the waiting room who was "neglecting her own child." Instead, he had targeted respectable Ruby Turpin.[11]

---

10. Ibid., 507.
11. Ibid., 502.

Ruby Turpin struggled mightily against the judgment God's grace had leveled against her. She was too respectable to be numbered with "trash." She told God, "If you like trash better, go get yourself some trash. . . . You could have made me trash."[12]

Finally, Ruby Turpin heard the message of grace as the liberating good news it is supposed to be. Like the apostle Paul, she surrendered to the God of all grace. After an afternoon of struggle, with her eyes fixed on her hogs "as if she were absorbing some abysmal life-giving knowledge," "she lifted her head" and "raised her hands from the side of the pen in a gesture hieratic and profound [priestly submission and worship]."[13] She had experienced what Philip Yancey says about God's amazing grace: "Grace does not excuse sin, but it treasures the sinner. True grace is shocking, scandalous. It shakes our conventions with its insistence on getting close to sinners and touching them with mercy and hope."[14]

With the afternoon sun now sinking "behind the tree line," Mrs. Turpin had a vision of a bridge leading up from earth toward heaven, and extending through a span of blazing fire. She saw moving along the bridge a throng of people ascending to heaven. There were large companies of "white trash." For the first time they had been made clean. There were bands of blacks dressed in white robes. There were also legions of "freaks and lunatics shouting . . . and leaping like frogs." Bringing up the rear of the procession was a large group of people Ruby knew. They were people like her and Claud who had always been respectable. She could tell by their shocked faces that their goodness and merits were burning away. The crickets in the surrounding woods were chirping as night descended. But all

---

12. Ibid., 507.

13. Ibid., 508.

14. Philip Yancey, *What's So Amazing about Grace?* Study Guide Edition (Grand Rapids: Zondervan, 1998), 153.

Ruby "heard were the voices of the souls climbing upward into the starry field and shouting hallelujah."[15]

Now, who is Mary Turpin? She is every person who in obedient repentance learns that "where sin abound[s], grace [can] much more abound" (Rom. 5:20, KJV) and who learns "while we were yet sinners, Christ died for us" (v. 8, KJV). She is every person who receives Jesus Christ, "who believe[s] in his name," and is given "power to become children of God" (John 1:12).

The most important question we will ever ask is, How will we respond to God's grace? Its source, its meaning, its power, and its reach are not in question. The epistle to the Ephesians repeatedly celebrates "the riches of [God's] grace which he lavished upon us" (1:7-8; 2:5, 7; 3:2, 7-8; 4:7; cf. 1 Pet. 1:3). By grace, Paul tells the Colossians, God has "delivered us from the dominion of darkness and transferred us to the kingdom of his beloved Son" (Col. 1:13; cf. Rom. 3:28).

God's grace is not a substance or a divine accumulation. It is God acting, being himself. Grace is God coming toward us, toward his creation, as faithful Creator and Redeemer. Grace is a verb, divine in character and action, as abundant as the "precious oil" that ran down Aaron's head, overflowed onto his beard, and soaked the collar of his robe (Ps. 133:2).

Two Critical Questions

First, will we by the Spirit's empowerment, and by gifted obedient faith, submit to being born anew through the Holy Spirit? Will we embrace God's judgment that when left to our own devices we are helplessly lost in trespasses and sin? The good news of the gospel of Jesus Christ is that by grace alone God can make all things new.

---

15. O'Connor, "Revelation," 508-9.

The *second* question is, Will we *begin* by grace through faith and *continue* day by day and moment by moment by grace through faith alone? One of the greatest dangers Christians face is thinking they can remain in God's favor by religious accomplishments, their own holiness.

The apostle Paul asked the Galatian Christians: "Are you so foolish? Having begun with the Spirit, are you now ending with the flesh?" (Gal. 3:3). They had heard and received the good news that by grace through faith they could place their trust in Jesus Christ, be forgiven of their sins, and delivered "from the present evil age" (1:4). But after Paul's departure, Judaizers appeared. They agreed that faith in Jesus Messiah was essential. But they believed faith was only the beginning. To be made complete, the Galatians would have to accept circumcision and abide by Torah restrictions.

The Galatians were in the process of deserting him who had called them into God's grace and were now "turning to a different gospel—not that there is another gospel" (vv. 6-7). Even if an angel comes from heaven and preaches a gospel contrary to the gospel of grace, "let him be accursed" (v. 8).

Paul wants the Galatians and us to understand that not only are we reconciled to God by faith in Jesus, but we will also continue our Christian discipleship by faith. "For freedom Christ has set us free; stand fast therefore, and do not submit again to a yoke of slavery" (5:1). Relying upon anything other than faith in Jesus Christ makes Christ "of no advantage" (v. 2).

Many people cannot identify with Ruby Turpin, the Galatian Christians struggling with legalism, or some Corinthian Christians who yielded to moral carelessness. Perhaps they have never heard of God's grace. Or perhaps they are like those in the Gospels such as Mary Magdalene, the tax collectors Zacchaeus and Matthew, the woman taken in adultery, and the Gadarene demoniac who thought themselves excluded from God's love until Jesus arrived. They are people Ruby Turpin lay awake at night thanking God "she wasn't like."

The amazing grace to which Ruby Turpin finally surrendered and into which she entered knows no strangers. Jesus the Good Shepherd graciously seeks all lost sheep—self-righteous Ruby Turpin and all the people "she wasn't like."

Two Enemies of Grace

The apostle Paul battled two enemies of grace: antinomianism and legalism.

Antinomianism

The term "antinomian" was coined by Martin Luther. It derives from two Greek words: *anti* (against) and *nomos* (law). "Antinomianism" means "against the law" or "no law." Because Christians are justified by grace through faith alone, or until they are, antinomians say, the law does not apply to them. This can take two forms.

John Wesley encountered the *first* form of antinomianism among the Moravians in England. They held that until a person knows with absolute certainty his or her standing before God, that person should not study the Scriptures, receive the Eucharist, or perform outward works such as relieving one's neighbor. The Eucharist was a privilege only for confident believers for whom all doubts had been extinguished; there were no degrees of faith. Seekers were supposed to be "still" and "quiet" until they were certain they had been born of God, made holy. Doing otherwise amounted to seeking salvation by works. By contrast, Wesley believed the ordinances of God, termed *means of grace*, while not meritorious, could aid one in coming to faith, to certainty. At least early on, the "Moravian" problem plagued some of Wesley's Methodists.

A *second* form of antinomianism holds that Christian freedom means freedom from the law, from practiced adherence to Christian ethics. If God is glorified by forgiving sins, then the more we sin, the more God forgives and the more he is glorified (Rom. 6:1-4). On the surface, antinomians of this sort are in one sense correct. However, they completely fail to see that God's grace sets us free not only *from* the law as the means by which we are reconciled to him but also *for* the law, for doing God's will as correctly expressed in the Ten Commandments and the standards of the New Testament.

The epistle of Jude says that antinomians of this form "pervert the grace of our God" (v. 4). They plagued the church in Corinth, doing what even pagans refused to do (1 Cor. 5:1-11). They ignored Jesus's words: "Do not think that I have come to abolish the Law or the Prophets; I have not come to abolish them but to fulfill them. For truly I tell you, until heaven and earth disappear, not the smallest letter, not the least stroke of a pen, will by any means disappear from the Law until everything is accomplished" (Matt. 5:17-18, NIV).

The apostle Paul asked the church in Rome, "Are we to sin because we are not under law but under grace?" He answered, "By no means! Do you not know that if you yield yourselves to any one as obedient slaves, you are slaves of the one whom you obey?" (Rom. 6:15-16). A person will either be a slave to sin, Paul says, or a slave to righteousness. "The whole point of the kingdom," says N. T. Wright, "is that God is putting all things right, restoring the human race to its proper role and dignity, and those who persist in styles of life that corrupt and destroy that genuine humanity cannot inherit it."[16]

---

16. Wright, *Paul: A Biography*, 251.

Antinomianism continues to plague the church. It is prevalent among Christians who believe impotence before sin has priority over God's ability to transform believers in the image of Jesus Christ. By boasting of being sinners they think they protect justification by grace through faith alone. They ignore that justification must issue into the sanctification of all life. They undercut the "fruit of the Spirit" as the normal result of God's operative grace. They do this in favor of a misunderstood and misdirected "justification" that proceeds no further. The boast of being a "sinner" ignores the entire eighth chapter of Romans. Methodist theologian Geoffrey Wainwright observes that "resignation to the 'inevitability' of sin risks making it innocuous and thereby opens the door to antinomianism."[17]

Protestant leaders, including Martin Luther, Philip Melanchthon, John Calvin, and John Wesley, battled antinomianism. John Calvin spoke of the "third use of the law" applicable to "believers in whose hearts the Spirit of God already flourishes and reigns." "Actuated by the Spirit," the law becomes "the best instrument for enabling them daily to learn with greater truth and certainty what [the] will of the Lord is which they aspire to follow, and to confirm them in this knowledge."[18]

Legalism

Legalism, also known as moralism, is the opposite of antinomianism. It places a premium upon works and obedience to laws in numerous forms, including the Ten Commandments. Legalism may be the most subtle abuse of grace faced by Christians. Moralists hear God's call to a

---

17. Geoffrey Wainwright, *Doxology: The Praise of God in Worship, Doctrine, and Life* (New York: Oxford University Press, 1980), 132.

18. John Calvin, *The Institutes of the Christian Religion*, trans. Henry Beveridge (Edinburgh: Calvin Translation Society, 1845), bk. 2, ch. 7, sec. 12, CCEL, http://www.ccel.org/ccel/calvin/institutes.pdf.

transformed life and seek to obey. The problem arises when supposed progress becomes "meritorious"; it becomes the "reason" a Christian should be considered God's friend and Jesus's disciple. The subtlety of this temptation is that it appears as faithful obedience when in fact it has become the meritorious basis for fellowship with Jesus. Without realizing it, Ruby Turpin was an ambassador for this form of legalism.

Legalism is life lived "according to the flesh" just as surely as idolatry is life "according to the flesh." *Sarx* (Gk., "flesh"), as Paul uses the term when referring to sin (e.g., Rom. 7:5; 8:1-9; Gal. 5:13, 16-21), does not mean *sōma* (Gk., "fleshly body"). *Flesh*, as it relates to human life under sin's sway, can include anything in God's creation treated as the source of life, as ultimate, as idolatrous. Legalism relies upon a particular form of *sarx*—accomplishments. It is the opposite of living "according to the Spirit." The Messiah's people must "worship God in spirit, and glory [boast] in Christ Jesus, and put no confidence in the flesh" (Phil. 3:3).[19]

Another shade of legalism currently plagues many Christians. In their rightful emphasis upon transformation and the holy life, they minimize God's grace by minimizing the need for regular confession and forgiveness. Unless they have grievously trespassed against God, they see no reason for confession. When one does not live by grace through faith alone, when holiness is egocentric instead of Christocentric, when one does not practice honesty before God, others, and oneself, confession before God and others becomes an enemy of holiness.

---

19. Wright explains that in Philippians 3:2, instead of using the word for circumcision (*peritomē*), Paul uses a Greek word (*katatomēn*), which means "the act of making a cut in something," "mutilation." Those who go around insisting that Christians be circumcised are no better than pagan cult members who want to make knife marks on people's flesh. Paul has used a pun to make his point. Wright, *Paul: A Biography*, 276.

To the contrary, the privilege and responsibility of confession that grace offers should become a daily Christian practice. Corporate and individual confession is at home in an atmosphere of grace. It evidences confidence in God and honest self-examination. It *complements* Christian witness and holiness and places Christians and congregations in the company of Jesus.

The privilege and responsibility of confession provided by grace should never be confused with antinomianism or retardation of growth in the image of Christ. Instead, it takes full account of living and working in a world where redemption has yet to be completed. In explaining what 1 John says about confession of sin (1:5–2:6), Wright and Bird say that while the age to come, the new creation, has already been launched, and believers share in its life through the Spirit, the "old age of sin and death" overlaps it in many ways, as the "not yet." While those born of God do not "habitually sin" (3:5, 9), in obedient faith they readily confess their failures to approximate, to embody, to bear witness to *new creation*, and confidently receive God's promised forgiveness.[20] Any form of Christian holiness that excludes John's honesty and instruction thereby excludes God's grace and forgiveness. Corporate Christian worship should encourage and make a place for the confession that grace requires and provides.

The Indicative and the Imperative

Is the Christian life an unending struggle against some form of legalism or antinomianism? Must a Christian endlessly bounce between impotence and self-righteousness? What does grace accomplish and what does it require?

---

20. Wright and Bird, *New Testament in Its World*, 806.

What God has provided through Jesus Christ comes first; then comes the imperative, the command. What is commanded is an outworking, an expression of what God has given (Rom. 12:10-16).

The New Testament's answer rests in a critical distinction between two Greek verb moods, the *indicative* and the *imperative*.

The Indicative

The indicative mood takes numerus forms. In general it is used to make a true assertion. It declares or creates a state of being. For example, "God so loved the world" makes a declaration about something God chose to do; it is an established reality. The indicative can also appear in the form of a question: "But he answered them, 'You see all these, do you not?'" (Matt. 24:2). The assumed answer is, "Yes." The disciples had just pointed out the buildings. It can also sound hypothetical: "But if I build up again those things which I tore down, then I prove myself a transgressor" (Gal. 2:18). Paul is not about to "tear down" what he earlier "built up." Most often in the New Testament the indicative mood appears as something God has accomplished in Christ. "He is the source of your life in Christ Jesus, whom God made our wisdom, our righteousness and sanctification and redemption" (1 Cor. 1:30; cf. 2 Cor. 5:19; Gal. 5:1; Eph. 1:7; 2:1). The indicative is new life made possible by Christ, through the Holy Spirit in which "the whole fabric of human allegiance is set right."[21]

The Imperative

The *imperative* mood issues a command, a request, or a desire. "Be holy, because I am holy" (1 Pet. 1:16, NIV). "Stand fast therefore, and do not submit again to a yoke of slavery" (Gal. 5:1).

Especially in Paul, the imperative never precedes the indicative. What God has provided through Jesus Christ

---

21. Paul W. Meyer, *The Word in This World: Essays in New Testament Exegesis and Theology*, ed. John T. Carroll (Louisville, KY: Westminster John Knox Press, 2004), 121.

comes first; then comes the imperative, the command. What is commanded is an outworking, an expression of what God has given (Rom. 12:10-16). *New being* in Christ precedes and is expressed in *new doing* through the Holy Spirit (Rom. 8:2-4). This is true Christian freedom (in Christ) (Gal. 5:1). The order appears repeatedly. *Indicative*: "In him we have redemption through his blood, the forgiveness of our trespasses, according to the riches of his grace which he lavished upon us" (Eph. 1:7-8). *Imperative*: "I therefore, a prisoner for the Lord, beg you to lead a life worthy of the calling to which you have been called, with all lowliness and meekness, with patience, forbearing one another in love" (Eph. 4:1-2; cf. Rom. 12:1-2).

The indicative is now to be manifest, declared through the imperative (cf. Titus 2:11-14; 3:3-8). It involves "living out the pattern of the Messiah" (cf. Eph. 2:11-22; 4:22-24; 5:1-2; 1 Pet. 1:13-21).[22] The Christian imperative always bears witness to the indicative, never to itself ("adorn the doctrine of God our Savior" [Titus 2:10]). It is rooted in and empowered by the indicative. Christian ethics "is atonement in action."[23] It is *cruciform*, cross-shaped discipleship—participating in Jesus's own death and resurrection.[24] Augustine captured the relationship in his beautiful prayer: "My whole hope is in thy exceeding great mercy and that alone. Give what thou commandest and command what thou wilt."[25]

---

22. Wright, *Paul: A Biography*, 336. "The death and resurrection of Jesus is, for Paul . . . a pattern that must be woven into every aspect of church life" (336).

23. Michael J. Gorman, *The Death of the Messiah and the Birth of the New Covenant* (Eugene, OR: Cascade Books, 2014), 55.

24. "In the Bible behaviors or practices are never discussed or demanded in a vacuum. They are always part of a relational, or covenantal, framework. As the initiator of the covenant, God makes both promises and demands within that covenant. . . . The people with whom God covenants make promises in return, particularly promises to fulfill the demands of the covenant." Ibid., 81-82.

25. Augustine, *Confessions*, bk. 10, ch. 29, sec. 40, in *Confessions and Enchiridion*, trans. and ed. Albert C. Outler (Philadelphia: Westminster Press, 1955),

In the Gospel of John, the indicative and the imperative are tightly woven in mutual love. "If you love me, you will keep my commandments" (John 14:15; cf. 14:21). The Son's loving obedience to his Father is the model. Just as the Son "speaks the Father's word and does His works, so the disciples are loved by Christ and return His love in obedience; in doing so, they share His life, which manifests itself in doing His works." The Son does the works of the Father through His disciples.[26]

Conclusion

The Bible is far more focused on God's efforts and power to redeem than upon sin's ability to alienate and enslave. Absolutely no corner of human life is excluded from God's love, his grace, his desire to redeem. The uniform conviction of the New Testament is that in Christ, God the Father inaugurated new creation meant for everyone. With confidence everyone can pray, "Just as I am, without one plea, / But that Thy blood was shed for me."[27]

By God's grace, everyone can with Ruby Turpin join "the voices of the souls climbing upward into the starry field and shouting hallelujah!"[28]

CCEL, http://www.ccel.org/ccel/augustine/confessions.pdf.

26. Dodd, *Interpretation of the Fourth Gospel*, 195-96.

27. Charlotte Elliott, "Just as I Am," in *Sing to the Lord* (Kansas City: Lillenas, 1993), no. 343.

28. O'Connor, "Revelation," 509.

| SIX | # Released from Perfection / Called to Perfection |

Of the many literary devices employed by Shakespeare, one of his most puzzling is *paradox*. A paradox is a statement that sounds like a contradiction but is actually true. Paradoxes were popularly used in Renaissance literature to challenge conventional thought. In *Hamlet*, act 3, scene 4, Hamlet declares, "I have to be cruel, only to be kind." In *Macbeth*, act 1, scene 1, a first witch asks, "When shall we three meet again?" A second witch answers, "When the battle's lost and won." Together they cry, "Fair is foul, and foul is fair."

In the Bible, a central paradox makes Shakespeare's use of paradox sound like child's play. God who is perfect requires humans who are fallible to be perfect just as he is perfect. Jesus, who understood what it means to be human, issued the summons: "Therefore you shall be perfect, just as your Father in heaven is perfect" (Matt. 5:48, NKJV).

The Tyranny of Perfection

If ever a tyrannical and contradictory command were issued to humans, Jesus's command must qualify as a prime candidate. By definition it seems impossible and oppressive. God is God. Being perfect is part of what it means to be God. The psalmist recognized this: "As for God, his way is perfect: The LORD's word is flawless" (Ps. 18:30, NIV).

By contrast, humans are human. Essentially, we are finite, inherently prone to many kinds of error, and woefully lacking in strength and knowledge.

We can do many things. Being perfect as God is perfect is not one of them. Still, the oppressive and unrealistic command stands. "Therefore you shall be perfect, just as your Father in heaven is perfect" (Matt. 5:48, NKJV). The command seems inescapable, for to disobey God is sinful.

The command is repeated throughout the Old and New Testaments. When Abraham was age ninety-nine, "the LORD appeared to him and said, 'I am God Almighty; walk before me faithfully and be blameless'" (Gen. 17:1, NIV). Paul tells the Christians in Rome that they should obey the will of God, which is "good and acceptable and perfect" (Rom. 12:2).

Paul's desire for the Colossian Christians is that they "stand perfect and complete in all the will of God" (Col. 4:12, KJV). James weighs in; his readers are to be "perfect and entire, wanting nothing" (James 1:4, KJV). James describes the "perfect" Christian. When a person's language is completely free of offense, he is "perfect" (3:2).

"Human perfection" is one of the most troublesome, oppressive, and disruptive concepts imaginable. Possessing reflective ability, humans can imagine overcoming the chasm between what "is" and what conceivably "might be." But achievement is impossible. It seems God's commandment about perfection has maliciously trapped humans in a damnable dilemma. If we ignore the commandment, we sin. If we try but fail, we sin. If we try to become perfect and claim to have succeeded, we commit the sins of dishonesty and hubris. "Perfect" people can become oppressive disrupters in families, nations, and churches. Their failure broadcasts its consequences in every direction.

Before the New Testament era ends, "perfection" is threatening the church. The Galatians are being plagued by "perfect" Christians from Jerusalem who want to teach the Galatians how to become "perfect" (Gal. 3:1-5). Corinthian Christians already know quite well how to become "perfect." It comes by being attached to a super-preacher or an apostle (1 Cor. 1:10-17). Others have decided it comes by possessing superior gifts of the Spirit not available to other church members (12:1-26). A few thought perfection came through Greco-Roman social status (1:26-37). James lectures some "perfect" church members who can't discipline their tongues, and others who think they can "fulfil the royal law" while making poor visitors "sit at [their] feet" (1:26–2:8). And Jude warned against so-called perfect supersaints who cause "divisions" in the church but who are in fact bankrupt "of the Spirit" (Jude v. 19).

Perfection often left an unsavory record in church history. Monasteries, established for perfecting the soul, became so corrupt that a major tenth-century reform effort led by the Benedictine Order (the Cluniac Reforms) became necessary. After the sixteenth-century Protestant Reformation, a desire for the "perfection" of theological systems yielded an almost endless array of denominations. The brutal European Wars of Religion (sixteenth, seventeenth, and early eighteenth centuries) resulted from conflicts between Catholics and Protestants over who "perfectly" understood the Christian faith.

Some of history's most devastating social disruptions have resulted from a philosopher or visionary who had supposedly figured out how to perfect the human race. Karl Marx (1818-83) was confident that if humankind could develop into a classless society, all exploitation of the proletariat workers by bourgeois industrialists would cease. Heaven on earth, minus God, would gloriously descend. That promised "perfection" eventually left millions of people dead or enslaved. The list of religious figures who tried their hand at social perfection is almost endless.

Efforts to become "perfect as God is perfect" lead to paralyzing, disorienting defeat for many, immobilization for some, and unbridled arrogance in others. The effort is inevitably divisive among churches, families, and nations. "Perfection" needs clear boundaries between achievers and slackers. Perfect people desperately need to protect and display their gains. They need boundary markers between themselves and the losers. Markers can be derived from religion, class, race, gender, nationality, and economic accomplishments. In religion, perfection creates a culture of "winners" and "losers" and finds ways to keep "losers" at a safe distance.

Perfection can become psychologically, morally, and religiously paralyzing. It can cause stress, anxiety, depression, and other mental health problems. Many live as cripples because they can never be "good enough." Try as they might, the chasm between "is" and "ought" seems to widen.

Perhaps, with due respect for Jesus, the time has come for honest and healthy people to abandon the illusory pursuit of perfection—to accept failures and be done with it. Perhaps they should borrow the words of Ivan in Dostoyevsky's *The Brothers Karamazov*: "It's not God that I don't accept," Ivan told his brother Alyosha. I just "respectfully return Him the ticket."[1] For individual and social well-being, it might be time to be *released from perfection*, time to "return the ticket" to the unrealistically commanding God.

Unless . . .

---

1. Fyodor Dostoyevsky, "Rebellion," ch. 4 in bk. 5 of *The Brothers Karamazov*, 1880, trans. Constance Garnett (New York: Lowell Press, 1912; repr., Project Gutenberg, 2009), https://www.gutenberg.org/files/28054/28054-h/28054-h.htm.

The New Testament Call to Perfection

Unless we have somehow completely misunderstood Jesus and the New Testament writers. In fact, such has happened. A major course correction in our understanding is required.

The correction begins with language. The English language is rich in many ways. But the term "perfect" is not one of them. It derives from the Latin *perfectio* and implies moral flawlessness and absolute perfection. It is incapable of explaining the various New Testament terms and shades of meaning for "perfect." We will examine the words. Space does not permit an examination of Hebrew terms for perfection.[2]

First, keep in mind *everything* said in the New Testament about Christians being perfect or perfected is grounded in the Great Commandment. "'Love the Lord your God with all your heart and with all your soul and with all your mind.' This is the first and greatest commandment. And the second is like it: 'Love your neighbor as yourself'" (Matt. 22:37-39, NIV). *Second,* New Testament language about being perfect must be heard within the context of how the Holy Spirit is patiently applying the fruit of Christ's life, death, resurrection, and ascension to our lives. *Third,* understand perfection within the context of God's enabling grace, never with reference to human accomplishments. Any perception of perfection not thoroughly conditioned by grace will likely yield either frustration and defeat or unjustifiable boasts. *Fourth,* the inaugurated kingdom of God has yet to be consummated. It is both *already* and *not yet* in the church, the world, and in each of us. In the New Testament there is a yearning and creative "eschatological tension" (Rom. 8:22-24; Phil. 3:12-16; 1 Pet. 1:13; 1 John

---

2. For an examination of Hebrew terms for perfection, see William M. Greathouse, *Wholeness in Christ: Toward a Biblical Theology of Holiness* (Kansas City: Beacon Hill Press of Kansas City, 1998), 29-32.

3:2).[3] Christians *have been* saved, *are being* saved, and *will be* saved. We are works in progress. Believers are engaged in what Michael Gorman calls an "apocalyptic battle" against spiritual forces of evil (Eph. 6:12; 2 Cor. 10:4).[4] *Fifth*, in the New Testament perfection is inseparable from the Christian disciplines.

All New Testament commands for Christians rest upon God's love and *responsible* grace. Ours is a heavenly Father, not a heavenly tyrant. His goals for us, including his corrections, consistently express divine love. New Testament theologian Ben Witherington III states, "As the prophets told us, God requires of us that we reflect the divine character—to do justice, to love kindness and to walk humbly with our God. What God requires of us, he enables us to do, so that in small measure we may reflect the virtuous and free character of our God."[5]

Teleios

When Jesus says "You, therefore, must be perfect, as your heavenly Father is perfect" (Matt. 5:48), the Greek word used is *teleios*. The root is *telos*, which means "complete," "aim," "purpose," the "principal end." It can also mean a "toll" or "tax." *Teleios* means "complete in all its parts," "full grown," and "of full age." It applies especially to the completeness of Christian character. When Jesus prays that his disciples will become "perfectly one" (John 17:23), he is praying to the Father that they will accomplish or fulfill (*teleioō*) his will or plan for them.

The word is used in Matthew 19:21 when Jesus tells the rich young ruler, "If you would be perfect, go, sell what

---

3. Imbelli, *Rekindling the Christic Imagination*, 17.

4. Michael J. Gorman, *Becoming the Gospel: Paul, Participation, and Mission* (Grand Rapids: Eerdmans, 2015), 64.

5. Ben Witherington III, "The Freedom of God and the Free Will of Human Beings," *Ben Witherington* (blog), June 10, 2008, http://benwitherington.blogspot .com/2008/06/freedom-of-god-and-free-will-of-human.html.

you possess and give to the poor, and you will have treasure in heaven; and come, follow me."

Paul says that Christ is the "end [*telos*] of the law, that everyone who has faith may be justified" (Rom. 10:4). He doesn't mean that the Torah is "terminated" or "abolished" by Christ but that the righteousness that comes through trust in Christ was God's intent or goal for the Torah—the holy, just will of God (7:12, 14)—all along.[6]

In Romans 12:2, Paul uses *teleios* when he appeals to the Roman Christians: "Do not be conformed to this world but be transformed by the renewal of your mind, that you may prove what is the will of God, what is good and acceptable and perfect [*teleion*]." His goal for the Colossian Christians is that they become "mature (*teleion*) in Christ" (Col. 1:28). He urges holy completion in Christ as Christ's death provides (vv. 20-22). This has nothing to do with human achievement or flawlessness.

In Jesus's High Priestly Prayer (John 17:1-26), he prays that his disciples "may become perfectly one" (v. 23). The word is *teleioō*. It means "to bring to an end," "to complete," "to perfect." This form of *telos* is often used in Hebrews: 2:10; 5:9; 7:19; 9:9; 10:1; 11:40. In 12:22-23 the writer says Christians "have come to . . . a judge who is God of all, and to the spirits of just men made perfect." In Philippians 3:12 Paul uses *teleioō* to speak of what he has *not* yet obtained as a Christian: "Not as though I had already attained, either were already perfect" (KJV). James says through works, Abraham's faith was "made perfect" (James 2:22, KJV).

James uses *teleios* in 1:4, 17, and 25 to describe the full effect of remaining steadfast. All the "perfect" gifts come from the "Father of lights," and the Christian "law of liberty" is "perfect" (1:17, 25, KJV). John H. Elliott shows that for James, perfection involves integration of the whole

---

6. Meyer, *Word in This World*, 88.

person—thought, speech and action—in compliance with the "royal law of freedom" (see v. 25). A *complete* law of liberty (faith activated in love [2:1-26]) requires *complete* (*teleios*) persons who are receptive to the *complete* blessings that come from God above (1:17).[7]

Aristotle usually taught that there are four "causes" for things. Examples are wheels or drinking cups: (1) the material cause (made of something), (2) the efficient cause (crafted by someone), (3) the formal cause (the craftsperson has a form in mind), and (4) the final or *telic* (from *telos*) cause—directed toward an end or purpose. The wheel is "perfect" if it achieves its intended purpose, its design, even if it has chips in its wood or metal.

What is God's intended purpose or goal for Christians? It takes the entire New Testament to answer the question. But in summary, the intended purpose or goal of the "Master Craftsman" is that as "new creations" we reflect God's glory through transformation in the image of Christ. *When* and *as* that happens, a Christian is "perfect." And we are a "work in progress" (see Eph. 1:15-22; Phil. 3:12-16). Through the Holy Spirit, Christ will continue to refine (to perfect) his work until "the perishable puts on the imperishable, and the mortal puts on immortality" (1 Cor. 15:54). Until then, Jesus's disciples must be "steadfast, immovable, always abounding in the work of the Lord, knowing that in the Lord your labor is not in vain" (v. 58). Remember Paul's counsel to the Corinthian Christians is given to the most troublesome and conflicted church in the New Testament. They certainly had not fully achieved God's design for them. Nevertheless, Paul addresses them as "sanctified in Christ Jesus" and "called to be saints" (1:2).

The kingdom of God has been inaugurated and is proceeding toward its consummation. To be complete in Christ

---

7. Elliott, "Epistle of James," 117.

involves participating in "new creation" now (2 Cor. 5:17) and advancing toward the time when Christ "delivers the kingdom to God the Father" (1 Cor. 15:24). *Teleios* is both *already* and *not yet* (Phil. 3:7-16).

Katartizō

The word *katartizō* is also used for perfection. It can mean "to mend [what has been broken or torn]," "to repair, equip, complete," "to put in order, arrange, and adjust." Ethically, *katartizō* means "to strengthen," "to perfect," "to complete," and "to make one what he or she ought to be."

Jesus saw James and John "mending their nets" and called them to be his disciples (Matt. 4:21). *Katartizō* is used in Luke 6:40: "The disciple is not above his master: but every one that is perfect shall be as his master" (KJV). Paul used the word to instruct the Galatians about a fallen brother. "Brothers and sisters, if someone is caught in a sin, you who live by the Spirit should *restore* that person gently" (Gal. 6:1, NIV, emphasis added; cf. 1 Pet. 5:10; cf. 1 Thess. 3:10).

Holoklēria

A term for perfect used only once is *holoklēria*. It means "completeness," "unimpaired in body," "sound-ness," "integrity," and "wholeness." It can also mean "good health." Through Peter and John's ministry, a man lame from birth was healed in the temple. Peter told the crowd that faith in Jesus Christ has given the man "perfect sound-ness" (Acts 3:16, KJV).

Plēroō

Plēroō is used often. It means "to make full," "to complete," "to consummate," and "to bring to realization." The Lord tells the church in Sardis, "I have not found thy works perfect before God" (Rev. 3:2, KJV; cf. Matt. 2:17; Acts 1:16).

Artios

When Paul tells Timothy why studying the Scriptures is profitable, he uses the Greek word *artios*. The term means "complete," "perfect of its kind," "suitable," "exactly fitted." "All scripture is inspired by God and profitable for teaching, for reproof, for correction, and for training in righteousness, that the man of God may be *complete*, equipped for every good work" (2 Tim. 3:16-17, emphasis added).

Epiteleō

Paul chides the Galatians who are in danger of being deceived by the Judaizers: "Are you so foolish? After beginning by means of the Spirit, are you now trying *to finish* by means of the flesh?" (Gal. 3:3, NIV, emphasis added). He uses the word *epiteleō*, which means "to complete," "to accomplish."

Each term for "perfection" has its own context, application and distinct shading. However, the theme of wholeness according to purpose runs throughout. We hear of divine intention and enabled obedience. We also hear of responsibility. None of the terms permit spiritual sloth or carelessness. We hear nothing of freedom from error or not needing correction. All six terms are bathed in the enabling grace of God. Because of the Spirit's indwelling presence, New Testament writers can call Christians to *blamelessness* (Acts 24:16; 1 Cor. 1:8; Eph. 1:4; 5:27; 2 Pet. 3:14). Confidence in God's powerful love is the source of Christian hope and confidence (Rom. 8:26-39).

Christians are "blessed . . . with every spiritual blessing in Christ" so they may be "holy and blameless in his sight" (Eph. 1:3-4, NIV). Christ intends to present his church to himself as "holy and without blemish [*amōmos*]" (5:27; cf. Phil. 2:15; Col. 1:22; Heb. 9:14; 1 Pet. 1:19; Jude v. 24; Rev. 14:5). The Greek word *amōmos* means "blameless," "without blemish," "unblemished," "faultless." Paul gives thanks because the Lord Jesus Christ will "confirm" the Corinthians "to the end, *blameless* on the day of our Lord Jesus Christ" (1 Cor. 1:8, NASB, emphasis added). He tells the Colossians they have been reconciled to Christ through his crucifixion in order that Christ may present them "holy and *blameless* and beyond reproach" (Col. 1:22, NASB, emphasis added). Peter exhorts his readers to be "blameless" (2 Pet. 3:14, NASB) as they await the "day of God" (v. 12, NASB). He uses the word *amōmētos*, which means "unblemished." Holiness and godliness through the enabling, gracious work of God provide the meaning for "blameless."

Conclusion

All language about Christian perfection in the New Testament is saturated by God's enabling grace. It entails active obedience made possible by the Holy Spirit. It has nothing to do with flawlessness, human achievement, tyrannous perfectionism, or a completion of pilgrimage. It involves the lifelong process of being *recapitulated* to Christ, who in the fullness of time will "gather together [Gk., "sum up"] in one all things in Christ" (Eph. 1:10, KJV).

Obedient discipleship, observes Fleming Rutledge, bears witness to what Christ has already accomplished, is now accomplishing, and will consummate at his kingdom's fulfillment.[8]

What has become of our apparent contradiction, our paradox? It has been resolved by turning away from the perfection that enslaves to the perfection in Christ that sets us free for victorious life in the Son (Gal. 5:1).

> *The King of love my shepherd is,*
> > *whose goodness faileth never.*
> *I nothing lack if I am his,*
> > *and he is mine forever.*

---

8. Rutledge, *Crucifixion*, 555.

. . . .

And so through all the length of days,
thy goodness faileth never;
Good Shepherd, may I sing thy praise
within thy house forever.[9]

116

RELEASED FROM PERFECTION / CALLED TO PERFECTION

9. H. W. Baker, "The King of Love My Shepherd Is" (1868), Hymnary.org, https://hymnary.org/text/the_king_of_love_my_shepherd_is.

SEVEN

The "Inflated" Elephant in Romans 7

His name is Ngonyama. He weighs more than eleven thousand pounds and stands over eleven feet tall. He has blocked the bridge that crosses the Tsendze River near the Mopani Rest Camp in the Kruger National Park, South Africa. Due to his long tusks, this huge bull elephant is known as a "big tusker."[1]

Beyond the Tsendze River lie the breathtaking vistas of the Kruger National Park. Visitors are anxious to continue their explorations. But no one in his right mind will try to push Ngonyama aside. Until he moves, explorations are over; Kruger National Park is closed.

The Elephant in Romans 7

In the New Testament there appears to be another and much more formidable "Ngonyama." The apostle Paul in Romans 7:14-24 seems to be describing normal Christian life. Discipleship appears to be characterized by an unavoidable and vicious internal conflict in which sin remains so powerful it blocks access to victorious Christian living. War within oneself (v. 23) seems to be a Christian's inescapable lot: "We know that the law is spiritual; but I am

---

1. Africa Adventures, "Large Elephant 'Ngonyama' Road Block," YouTube Video, 6:03, June 13, 2018, https://www.youtube.com/watch?v=hMbYnol1iFQ.

carnal, sold under sin. I do not understand my own actions. For I do not do what I want, but I do the very thing I hate" (vv. 14-15).

Then things appear to deteriorate: "I see in my members another law at war with the law of my mind and making me captive to the law of sin which dwells in my members. Wretched man that I am!" (vv. 23-24a).

By grace, Christians have begun their journey with Christ Jesus. They have been buried with Christ in baptism and have been "raised from the dead by the glory of the Father." They are supposed to "walk in newness of life" (6:4). They are instructed not to let "sin . . . reign in their mortal bodies." They must not "yield [their] members to sin as instruments of wickedness." Instead, they must "yield [themselves] to God as [people] who have been brought from death to life" (vv. 12-13).

All this sounds inviting. But there stands that *unyielding elephant.* "I do not understand my own actions. For I do not do what I want, but I do the very thing I hate" (7:15). "I can will what is right, but I cannot do it. For I do not do the good I want, but the evil I do not want is what I do" (vv. 18-19).

Christians can peer into Romans 8, which seems to describe a different pattern for Christian life. "The law of the Spirit of life in Christ Jesus has set me free from the law of sin and death" (v. 2). Christians are now supposed to freely "walk not according to the flesh but according to the Spirit" (v. 4). They are supposed to "set their minds," unconflicted, "on the things of the Spirit" (v. 5). By the Spirit they are to "put to death the deeds of the body" (v. 13) because they are now "led by the Spirit of God" as "children of God" and as "co-heirs with Christ" (vv. 14, 17).

But wait! There stands that *defiant elephant* in Romans 7. "I am carnal, sold under sin. I do not understand my own actions. For I do not do what I want, but I do the very thing I hate. . . . I can will what is right, but I cannot do it. For I do not do the good I want, but the evil I do not want is what I do" (vv. 14-15, 18-19). Nothing in the text tells us how to remove the "Big Husker"!

Incurably gnawing inside Paul's "members" is a warring law that obstructs full obedience to God's will. Paul, the Christian, is a "wretched man" indeed (v. 24)! And the grand promises of victorious Christian life in Romans 8, free from internal conflict, are inaccessible. They stand as plaguing illusions, titillating mirages for thirsty Christians.

Guardians of the Elephant

An impressive line of great Christian teachers has confirmed the elephant's reality and imposing permanence. The elephant, they assure us, fixes the parameters for Christian life.

Three of these are Augustine of Hippo (354–430), Martin Luther (1483–1546), and John Calvin (1509-64). We will return to the apostle Paul after we examine their teachings.

Augustine of Hippo underwent a change of heart regarding Romans 7:14-24. First he believed the person Paul describes refers to Paul before he was converted, "a man put under the law, not yet under grace."[2] Augustine did not want the description to be understood as "arising from the person of the apostle who was already spiritual." But after reading some "eloquent divines whose authority moved him," Augustine changed his mind. He decided Paul is speaking of himself as an apostle when he says, "The law is spiritual; but I am carnal" (v. 14).

---

2. Augustine, *Retractationes*, trans. Meredith Freeman Eller (Boston: Boston University Graduate School, 1946), 166, Internet Archive, https://archive.org /details/retractationesof00elle.

Augustine changed partly in opposition to the Pelagians, who denied the doctrine of original sin. Augustine came to believe the language in Romans 7:14-24 "is better understood of a spiritual man already established under grace." The flesh and the spirit are at war with each other because of "the body of the flesh," which is not yet spiritual. But it "will be in the resurrection of the dead." Until then, Christians are in constant conflict with the "lust of the flesh." They are never free "from those impulses which they resist by struggling." The battle is between the spirit, on the one hand, and concupiscence (lust) and passion, on the other. Thankfully, Christians "will not possess those impulses in that life where 'death will be swallowed up in victory' [1 Cor. 15:54]."[3]

Martin Luther taught that by grace alone God freely gives Christ to us and pours the Holy Spirit and his blessings upon believers. God's gifts and the Holy Spirit must be received daily. But, explains John Dillenberger, according to how Luther reads Romans 7:14-23, even the gifts and the Holy Spirit "will be incomplete, for the old desires and sins still linger in us." They "strive against the Spirit." Nevertheless, "grace is sufficient to enable us to be accounted entirely and completely righteous in God's sight."[4]

In Romans 7, according to Luther, Paul is explaining how flesh and spirit contend with each other in our hearts. The term "law" is applied to "the spirit and the flesh because . . . the flesh strive[s] and struggle[s] and rages[s] against the spirit." The flesh "insists on its own way. This wrangling continues within us as long as we live; more in some, less in others." Our "complete self" as Christians

---

3. Ibid., 167.

4. Martin Luther, "Preface to the Epistle of St. Paul to the Romans," 1522, in *Martin Luther: Selections from His Writings*, ed. John Dillenberger (Garden City, NJ: Doubleday, 1961), 23.

"consists of both elements: spirit and flesh; we fight with ourselves until we become wholly spiritual."[5]

John Calvin wrote that in Romans 7:14-24 Paul "sets before us an example [of] a regenerate man, in whom the remnants of the flesh are wholly contrary to the law of the Lord, while the spirit would gladly obey it."[6] The flesh is what a person "brings from the womb." It is nature as corrupted, sinful. The flesh "neither tastes nor desires anything but what is gross and earthly. Spirit, on the contrary, is renewed nature, which God forms anew after his own image."[7] It is "the newness which is wrought in us" as a "gift of the Spirit."[8] Flesh by itself is "entirely controlled by the power of sin."[9] The carnal, unregenerate person "rushes into sin with the whole propensity of his mind."[10]

But, Calvin says, the unregenerate person is not who Paul describes in Romans 7:14-24. The conflict "does not exist in man before he is renewed by the Spirit of God."[11] In his *own person* Paul is describing "the weakness of the faithful, and how great [that weakness] is."[12]

> The godly, . . . in whom the regeneration of God is begun, are so divided, that with the chief desire of the heart they aspire to God, seek celestial righteousness, hate sin, and yet they are drawn down to the earth by the relics of their flesh: and thus, while pulled in two ways, they fight against their own nature, and nature fights against them; and they condemn their sins, not

---

5. Ibid., 31.

6. John Calvin, *Commentary on Romans*, trans. and ed. John Owen (Edinburgh: Calvin Translation Society, 1849), comm. on Rom. 7:14, CCEL, https://ccel.org/ccel/c/calvin/calcom38/cache/calcom38.pdf.

7. Ibid.

8. Ibid.

9. Ibid.

10. Ibid., comm. on Rom. 7:15.

11. Ibid.

12. Ibid.

only as being constrained by the judgment of reason, but because they really in their hearts abominate them, and on their account loathe themselves. This is the Christian conflict between the flesh and the spirit of which Paul speaks in Galatians 5:17.[13]

Division between the flesh and the spirit begins only in regeneration. We are made aware that "the relics of the flesh which remain, always follow their own corrupt propensities, and thus carry on a contest against the Spirit."[14] The flesh "has . . . its own will." But the chief desire, which ought to hold first place in the regenerate person, should be to do the will of the Spirit. The grace of the Holy Spirit "brings an agreement between the mind and the righteousness of the law."[15]

Nevertheless, "the flesh not only impedes the faithful, so that they cannot run swiftly, but it sets also before them many obstacles at which they stumble." To will to obey the Holy Spirit is "the readiness of faith." The Holy Spirit "so prepares the godly that they are ready and strive to render obedience to God." However, "their ability is not equal to what they wish." Because of this, Paul could not accomplish the good at which he aimed.[16] Paul is describing in general "the whole course of [the godly]."[17] Paul is describing the normal "Christian struggle," the "contest" between flesh and spirit in "pious souls."[18]

Well, there it is—the *imposing elephant* of Romans 7:14-24, as explained by these eminent teachers. Together they represent a major portion of Protestant Christianity.

---

13. Ibid.
14. Ibid.
15. Ibid.
16. Ibid., comm. on Rom. 7:18.
17. Ibid., comm. on Rom. 7:19.
18. Ibid., comm. on Rom. 7:22.

The *elephant*, they agree, is real and formidable. "Normal" Christian life should be understood as two laws incessantly warring in a Christian's members.

Nevertheless, Christians are much better off living with the *elephant* than are those entirely controlled by the lusts of the flesh. Furthermore, they can look forward to the afterlife when they will be set free from the tyrant that dwells in us (v. 18). God's grace, says Luther, should make us "joyful, high-spirited, and eager in our relations with God and with all mankind."[19]

Questions for Augustine, Luther, and Calvin

If Augustine, Luther, and Calvin are correct, and the *elephant* is as real and powerful as they believe, then much of what Paul says prior to Romans 7:14-24 makes no sense. "We know that our old self was crucified with [Christ] so that the sinful body might be destroyed, and we might no longer be enslaved to sin. For he who has died is freed from sin" (6:6-7). "Having been set free from sin, [you] have become slaves of righteousness" (v. 18). Slaves are not torn between two masters. "Now yield your members [Gk., *melē* (parts of the body)] to righteousness for sanctification [*hagiasmon* (holiness)]" (v. 19). "But now that you have been set free from sin and have become slaves of God, the return you get is sanctification [*hagiasmon* (holiness)]" (v. 22).

How are those statements to be reconciled with what Augustine, Luther, and Calvin describe as normal Christian life? Any rational person would conclude the two conflicting assessments—freedom or endless conflictive slavery—were either written by different persons or by the same person, who is then hopelessly conflicted and in no position to guide others intelligently.

---

19. Luther, "Preface," 24.

Deflating the Elephant

What if Paul is not conflicted? What if what he says in Romans 7:14-24 has been badly misunderstood? What if, upon closer examination, we were to discover that the *elephant* straddling Romans 7:14-24 is inflated rubber, *not a real elephant after all*?

Paul's Place in the Greco-Roman Social Structure

To correctly understand what Paul means in Romans 7:14-24, we must examine his "social location" [20] in Greco-Roman culture and what his level of education qualified him "to do."[21]

Where was Paul located?

He was a member of the retainer class. Luke portrays Paul at home in the presence of the governing class of Israelites *and* the Greco-Roman governing classes.

Scholars draw this conclusion in part because of Paul's knowledge and writings. He could write special kinds of letters. As a schoolboy he studied a curriculum known as progymnastic in which he learned the building blocks of composition and speech. These were essential for entering the civic arena. Only those of high social status would have had the resources, the social need, and the leisure for the kind of writing Paul learned to produce. Scholars observe that when Paul employs a particular form of rhetoric, he does so intentionally.

Scholars recognize in Romans 7:14-24 that Paul is deliberately using a particular form known as *prosopopoeia* to achieve a purpose his Roman audience would recognize. It is

---

20. Social location is one's position in a social system that reflects a worldview, a perception of how things work, what is real, where things belong, and how they fit together.

21. This section relies upon Jerome H. Neyrey, "The Social Location of Paul: Education as the Key," University of Notre Dame, https://www3.nd.edu/~jneyrey1/social-location.htm.

used when someone wants to speak or write "in character." It is "speech in character." Prosopopoeia is an example of deliberative rhetoric, used to persuade an audience to take (or not take) some action. When employing speech in character, a speaker adopts the voice of another person or object, but not of himself. An imaginary, absent, or even deceased person is represented as speaking and as providing another perspective. The speaker might project upon the fictional person (or thing) something unfavorable. The projected person then embodies the characteristics described.

New Testament scholar Ben Witherington III explains Paul's use of prosopopoeia in Romans 7:14-25 by first turning to 7:7-13.[22] Romans 7 "is not a new argument. It is a continuation of what Paul has been doing all throughout [Romans]."[23] What undergirds Romans 7 is Paul's insistence that all of us share a common humanity. Like Adam, we have all "fall[en] short of the glory of God" (Rom. 3:23).

The story of Adam is the "theme music that's playing in the background" of Romans 6 and 7. Romans 7 is often misunderstood because "we don't read" the chapter "rhetorically." Paul is using "speech in character" or "impersonation." He assumes "the persona of someone else"—namely, Adam and all those who are in Adam. Paul speaks in the first person as *that other* person. "The 'I' in Romans 7:7-13 . . . is not Paul." This is not his biography. The "I" is Adam, the same character the Roman Christians would have heard of in Roman 5:12-21.[24]

Why does the "I" not refer to Paul, as Augustine, Luther, and Calvin mistakenly believed, but instead to Adam? There are clues, "the most important of which is that this

---

22. Ben Witherington III, "Does Romans 7 Teach That Christians Will Continue Sinning?" YouTube Video, 8:47, posted by "Seedbed," July 29, 2014, https://www.youtube.com/watch?reload=9&v=aBXYp7cMblM.

23. Ibid.

24. Ibid.

'I' person says [he] existed before there was ever a law" (see 7:9). The only person who ever existed before God gave the law was Adam. God gave the commandment, and Adam violated it. When he did, "sin awoke, and I died" (see v. 9). Adam was the first person to experience the connection between sin and the wages of sin—death. So "what we have in Romans 7:7-13 is a retelling of the story of Adam and how the fall happened."[25]

Many believe in Romans 7:14-25 that Paul is describing a "normal" Christian struggling daily with the power of sin, which threatens to overwhelm the power of God's grace? Notice that in Philippians 3:4-6 "Paul talks about his past as a Pharisee." As to righteousness under the law, Paul was "blameless" (v. 6). He had a perfect score gained by keeping the law. "This doesn't sound like the Romans 7 person at all." Paul has a "robust" and perfectly "healthy conscience" about his behavior as a Pharisee. He was actually advancing beyond his peers.[26]

"So what is Romans 7:14-25 about?"[27] Who is this person who says, "I see in my members another law at war with the law of my mind and making me captive to the law of sin which dwells in my members" (v. 23)? This person "knows some of the truth but cannot do the truth. He is caught between knowing and doing. There is some kind of spiritual impediment in his life that prevents this."[28] Is Paul speaking for himself as a Christian? No, it isn't Paul and it is not "Christians in general either.[29] It is all those who are in Adam and outside of Christ. This is the descrip-

---

25. Ibid.

26. Ibid.

27. Ibid.

28. Ibid.

29. Recall that John Calvin said that Paul is "delineating in general the whole course of [the godly]." Calvin, *Commentary on Romans*, comm. on Rom. 7:19.

tion of a fallen person, maybe at the point of conversion struggling with sin."[30]

"Look at the context," Witherington insists. Just before Romans 7:7-25, in Romans 7:5-6 Paul says, "We were [this] way. But now we have been set free from the bondage to sin."[31] "That," Witherington says, "is exactly the message of Romans 8:1-2. When Paul wants to talk about Christians in Romans 8, . . . he says, 'There is . . . now no condemnation for those who are in Christ Jesus. For . . . the Spirit . . . has set [us] free from the [bondage to] sin and death' [vv. 1-2]." So we must contrast the person in Romans 7:7-25 with the person in Romans 8, the before and the after.[32]

This is not how Paul saw the world when still a Pharisee. "But since he has been in Christ, this is the way he views the lost world outside of Christ."[33]

Wright and Bird agree with Witherington, except unlike Witherington, who thinks Paul is speaking about Adam, they say Paul is speaking of Israel under the law. He is showing that embracing Torah as the way to life "merely increases the presence and power of sin."[34] Sin, as a powerful force, deceives the willing "I," causing it to believe law observance will produce life, when in fact the law is impotent to achieve this. "The demonic power of sin" uses the Mosaic law to effect the opposite of life, "the opposite of what its devoted adherents expect, even and especially when it is obeyed." The failure "manifests not only the sinister nature of sin itself [Rom. 7:11-13] but also how profoundly the religious self is 'sold' under [sin] and indeed possessed by it (vv. 14-20)."[35] Deceived by sin, death

---

30. Witherington, "Romans 7."
31. Ibid. Witherington is summarizing Romans 7:5-6.
32. Ibid.
33. Ibid.
34. Wright and Bird, *New Testament in Its World*, 519.
35. Meyer, *Word in This World*, 77.

Romans 7 must be understood correctly. If Paul is misunderstood, and then offered as the New Testament norm for Christian discipleship, a power is attributed to sin that effectively nullifies most, if not all, of the New Testament.

inevitably results. This is Paul's "own story." As a loyal Jew, he is a member of "Israel 'according to the flesh.'"[36] "The religious self is put in the wretched position of serving sin in its very [attempted] service to God."[37]

Paul says "what is needed is a power from [outside Torah], a gift that can create the capacity for freedom from fear and compulsion. Because that gift has been given [in Christ], Paul gives thanks in return" (see Rom. 7:24).[38] On behalf of us all—Jew and Gentile alike—God's own Son "[dealt] with sin as the law could not (8:3-4)."[39]

Conclusion

Romans 7 must be understood correctly. If Paul is misunderstood, and then offered as the New Testament norm for Christian discipleship, a power is attributed to sin that effectively nullifies most, if not all, of the New Testament. The gospel of Jesus Christ, the promise of redemption now, and the transforming power of the Holy Spirit are disfigured beyond recognition. Endless and taxing conflict, not victory through the Holy Spirit, becomes the pathetic offering of the risen Christ. He becomes a struggling competitor against sin, not the one who on the cross "disarmed the principalities and powers and made a public example of them, triumphing over them" (Col. 2:15). The best he offers is, "Be patient and trust your justification by grace; the raging internal conflict will cease after you die."

Given the way Paul is misunderstood, many Christians identify themselves primarily as "sinners." Spokespersons for a misunderstood Paul readily discredit Christians who believe the Holy Spirit equips Christians for holy

---

36. Wright, *Day the Revolution Began*, 283.
37. Meyer, *Word in This World*, 77.
38. Johnson, *Writings*, 328.
39. Meyer, *Word in This World*, 77.

living now. Armed with a "misunderstood Paul," they go forth to monitor Christian expectations according to the *elephant's* authority.

In the *elephant's* presence, the life of Christian holiness, to which Jesus's disciples are repeatedly called (Rom. 12:1-2; 2 Cor. 7:1; 1 Thess. 4:7; 5:23; Heb. 12:14; 1 Pet. 1:16), and for which provisions have been made (Rom. 8:11-17; 2 Cor. 7:1; 2 Pet. 1:3-11), becomes a haunting, mocking illusion. And Jesus Christ becomes an austere tyrant commanding what he cannot provide: "'And you shall love the Lord your God with all your heart, and with all your soul, and with all your mind, and with all your strength.' The second is this, 'You shall love your neighbor as yourself'" (Mark 12:30-31; 1 John 5:3).

At a practical level, for many Christians shaped by a misreading of Paul, spiritual paralysis is their Christian routine. One should read Ephesians 1:17-23 and then ask, Are "wars in one's members" what Paul expects as normal Christian life?

One must decide whether the *inflated elephant* in Romans 7:14-24 established the parameters of discipleship or whether Jesus, as Israel's Messiah, on the cross broke the power of the "present evil age" (Gal. 1:4) once and for all (Col. 2:15). One must ask, Has the powerful new life of the Messiah's resurrection been put into operation through the Holy Spirit, setting Jesus's people "free from sin in the present ([Rom.] 8:5-8) and free from death itself when they are raised from the dead (8:9-11)"?[40]

N. T. Wright has no doubt: the powers lose their hold when God forgives sin.[41] Realize what membership in the Messiah's family entails: crucifixion with Jesus (Gal. 5:24). Holiness, powered by the gospel of Jesus Christ, is required

---

40. Wright and Bird, *New Testament in Its World*, 519.
41. Wright, *Day the Revolution Began*, 241.

for crucified and resurrected members of the Messiah. For them the world has been crucified, and they have died to the world. The cross of Christ means Christians are now participants in the new creation. Conquest of the dark powers and the "present evil age" (Gal. 1:4) has happened, all because Christ "gave himself for our sins" (v. 4).[42]

The *inflated elephant* has been deflated. Romans 7 is put back in order. Now we can hear the good news. In Jesus Christ a new kind of power has been unleashed into the world. Equipped with the power of the Holy Spirit, Christians are to announce in their own victorious lives, and in proclamation, that *"a new reality has come to birth, that its name is 'forgiveness.'"*[43] A new kind of power has been turned loose into the world. The new power is "the chain-breaking, idol-smashing, sin-abandoning power called 'forgiveness,' called 'utter gracious love,' called *Jesus.*"[44]

What Witherington, Wright, Bird, and Johnson are saying about Romans 7:14-24 is fully compatible with the Christian "already and not-yet" as stated by Paul in Philippians 3:12: "Not that I have already obtained all this, or have already arrived at my goal, but I press on to take hold of that for which Christ Jesus took hold of me" (NIV).

---

42. Ibid., 244-45.
43. Ibid., 384.
44. Ibid.

Sin as Socially Structured

The English poet John Donne (1572–1631) wrote,

> No man is an island, entire of itself; every man is a
> piece of the continent, a part of the main. If a clod
> be washed away by the sea, Europe is the less, as well
> as if a promontory were, as well as if a manor of thy
> friend's or of thine own were: any man's death di-
> minishes me, because I am involved in mankind, and
> therefore never send to know for whom the bell tolls;
> it tolls for thee.[1]

Donne's meditation can also highlight the corporate
character of the church. Jesus made clear to Nicodemus that
as individuals we must be born anew in Christ by the work
of the Holy Spirit. Each of us must know we have been "delivered . . . from the dominion of darkness and transferred
. . . to the kingdom of [God's] beloved Son" (Col. 1:13). The
apostle Paul was explicit about his own redemption. "I live
by faith in the Son of God, who loved me and gave himself
for me" (Gal. 2:20). But we are "in Christ" only as members
of his body, the church (cf. Jesus's metaphor of the vine
and branches in John 15:1-11), of which he is the Head (1

---

1. John Donne, "Meditation XVII," in *Devotions upon Emergent Occasions* (1624;
repr., Ann Arbor, MI: University of Michigan Press, 1959; Project Gutenberg,
2007), 108-9, https://www.gutenberg.org/files/23772/23772-h/23772-h.htm.

Cor. 12:12-27; Col. 2:15-19). Paul says that the Father made Christ "head over all things for the church, which is his body, the fulness of him who fills all in all" (Eph. 1:22-23). Before his martyrdom, Cyprian (ca. AD 210-58), bishop of Carthage, told his persecuted flock in North Africa, "He can no longer have God for his Father, who has not the Church for his mother."[2]

Donne's meditation also calls attention to the fact that we become persons in and through complex social-moral structures. God created us as social beings, not as isolated atoms.

Customarily we think of sin as only something individuals commit. We usually think of the Adamic fall as affecting only individuals. However, the picture is much larger and more complex. In this chapter we consider sin as socially constructed and socially embedded. Examining sin from this perspective requires patience and self-examination. We *first* consider social structures. *Second*, we consider "orders of creation," their relationship to social structures, and how they can embody evil. *Third*, we examine how the Hebrews and Paul understood "person." *Fourth*, we look at how Paul understood the "powers."

Social Structures

Social structure refers to "social institutions and patterns of institutionalized relationships that compose society."[3] They embody, express, and enforce social norms and customs. Families, nations, economies, and churches affect our daily interactions. We begin to experience and to reflect

---

2. Cyprian, treatise I of *The Treatises of Cyprian*, "On the Unity of the Church," sec. 6, in vol. 5 of *Ante-Nicene Fathers*, ed. A. Cleveland Coxe (reprint of 1885 edition), CCEL, http://www.ccel.org/ccel/schaff/anf05.pdf.

3. Ashley Crossman, "The Concept of Social Structure in Sociology," ThoughtCo, updated June 28, 2019, https://www.thoughtco.com/social-structure-defined-3026594.

"within lived social worlds."[4] They are not always visible, nor are we always aware of their influence upon us. Social networks and all socioeconomic stratifications, including race, education, gender, and wealth, are embedded in them. One's "social location"[5] is placed within "social structures." In the words of theologian Miroslav Volf, all persons are socially "situated." But that doesn't eliminate the urgency of learning to live in harmony with and in respect for other "situated" persons and of learning from them.[6]

We can live in, help create, benefit from, or be harmed by social structures. During a seminar on the Holocaust I invited a Jewish attorney to speak. As a young Berliner he had lived through Adolf Hitler's rise to power. He regularly heard the Nazi propaganda and witnessed the creeping Nazi domination of Germany. He eventually realized he had to escape. So he and a friend fled, first to Switzerland and then to the United States. During their first night in Switzerland, he and his friend were in a bar when they heard someone loudly criticizing Adolf Hitler. He and his friend were so outraged that they started a brawl. He told us that only then did he, a Jew, realize how much Nazi ideology had shaped him.

An adequate examination of sin must include social structures. This might seem strange for Christians often formed by an individualistic, if not subjective, understanding of salvation. It can also appear strange to persons in modern and postmodern Western cultures influenced by the rise of individualism and individualistic psychology.

---

4. Michael Novak, *The Spirit of Democratic Capitalism* (New York: Touchstone, 1982), 61.

5. Sociologists define "social location" as one's position in a social system that reflects a worldview, a perception of how things work, what is real, where things belong, and how they fit together. Everyone is "socially located" in some way.

6. Miroslav Volf, *Exclusion and Embrace: A Theological Exploration of Identity, Otherness, and Reconciliation* (Nashville: Abingdon Press, 1996), 20.

The ancient Hebrews and the writers of the New Testament did not think of individuals as Westerners customarily do. So to understand sin and salvation we must question our modern understanding of the individual. How did the apostle Paul and other New Testament writers understand the relationship between persons and the social structures in which they lived?

Orders of Creation

Christian theologians often speak of "orders of creation" such as the family, in which social structures are formed and in which the human vocation is fulfilled. Lutheran theologian Carl E. Braaten defines the orders of creation as "the common structures of human existence, the indispensable conditions of the possibility of social life. Through these structures human beings are bound to each other in various relationships and mutual service."[7] This does not mean that God rigidly created all social structures but that the communal fabric of life is part of God's creation and care (cf. Col. 1:16). "The orders of creation are subject to the conditions of sin and death; nevertheless they are still the object of God's continuing and present act of creating" and redeeming.[8] "Faith in Jesus Christ," Braaten adds, "places all the orders of creation under the spotlight of the eschatological kingdom and rule of God."[9]

The apostle Paul recognized the state as an "order" established by God (Rom. 13:1-2). For Paul, says N. T. Wright, "A robust monotheism knows the Creator wants there to be [civic authorities]." They are responsible to God, "whether

---

7. Carl E. Braaten, "God in Public Life: Rehabilitating the 'Orders of Creation,'" pt. 2, sec. 1, *First Things* (December 1990), https://www.firstthings.com/article/1990/12/god-in-public-life-rehabilitating-the-orders-of-creation.

8. Ibid., pt. 2, sec. 4.

9. Ibid., pt. 2, sec. 6.

they know it or not."[10] Dutch theologian Hendrikus Berkhof observed, "In light of God's action [in the world] Paul perceived that mankind is not composed of loose individuals, but that structures, orders, forms of existence, or whatever they be called, are given us as part of creaturely life." They form part of the history of creation, fall, and preservation. They are included in reconciliation and the kingdom's consummation. Paul expressed these affirmations in the terms and concepts of his time.[11]

The apostle Peter instructed, "Submit yourselves for the Lord's sake to every human authority: whether to the emperor, as the supreme authority, or to governors, who are sent by him to punish those who do wrong and to commend those who do right" (1 Pet. 2:13-14, NIV).

Not all social structures fulfill God's intentions for the orders of creation. Their worth is judged by how well they serve human flourishing as intended by God. For example, do they promote justice for all persons as the Old Testament Prophets insisted, or are they "ordered" to grant privileges to the powerful at the expense of the poor, to men at the expense of women, and to one part of the globe at the expense of another? The Prophets were attentive to whether Israelite social structures were faithful to the covenant bond and the Ten Commandments (Isa. 1:17; Jer. 22:3; Amos 5:21-24; Zech. 7:9-10).

Individual and structured aspects of life must come under God's scrutiny. Both can either serve God's purposes or be distorted by sin. Failure to appreciate this restricts the range of sin's impact: the consequences of the fall. It reduces the range of human responsibility, grace, and redemption.

---

10. Wright, *Paul: A Biography*, 335.

11. Hendrikus Berkhof, *Christ and the Powers*, trans. John H. Yoder (Scottdale, PA: Herald Press, 1977), 66.

I was reared in the southern part of the United States during the Jim Crow era.[12] It emerged after Reconstruction, following the American Civil War. Jim Crow laws strictly governed relations between whites and persons of color. Through legislation and custom, Jim Crow laws segregated whites and blacks according to education, where one could live, employment, voting and government, entertainment, transportation, meals, and places of worship. Jim Crow constituted a comprehensive social structure legally designed to assure white social superiority at every level. For example, the JCPenney store had two water fountains, one for blacks and one for whites.

Black and white children were socialized in the Jim Crow structure. They attended separate schools, ate at different restaurants, and swam at separate beaches. Most whites embraced Jim Crow as rational, morally defensible, and socially binding. One could easily become a Christian without the moral legitimacy of Jim Crow ever being questioned. Martin Luther King Jr. said Southern churches were the most segregated places in the South. He grieved over white churches and clergy that had "adjusted to the status quo, standing as a taillight behind other community agencies rather than as a headlight leading men to higher levels of justice."[13]

Blacks were supposed to accept their "inferiority" as divinely ordained. They were to believe themselves inherently incapable of achieving successes available to most

---

12. Historians are not certain about the origin of the phrase "Jim Crow." For a full treatment of how the "Jim Crow" laws emerged, see C. Vann Woodward, *The Strange Career of Jim Crow* (New York: Oxford University Press, 1955).

13. Martin Luther King Jr., "Letter from a Birmingham Jail," April 16, 1963, The Martin Luther King Jr. Research and Education Institute, Stanford University, 15, http://okra.stanford.edu/transcription/document_images/undecided /630416-019.pdf. Note: The use of Jim Crow to illustrate sin as socially constructed should not be confused with critical race theory (CRT). I reject the premise and the ideology upon which CRT is predicated.

white people. When injustices were recognized, blacks were told to "wait." It always meant "never." Jim Crow segregation, said Martin Luther King, "distorted the soul and damaged the personality" of blacks and whites.[14]

Jim Crow was an illustration of *systemic evil* or *structured evil*. It was a largely comprehensive social system whose nature was to generate oppression for many and social benefits for others. Systemic evil "abducts" the orders of creation. Although fed by individuals, it acquires a life of its own. It develops the features of a "personal other" not immediately reliant upon its participants. However, the "spirit" or "self" of systems "can no more exist without concretion [to make concrete] in an institution or system or officeholder than the self can exist without a body."[15] Walter Wink observes that systemic evil is dependent not simply on the good or bad will of individuals but upon "a determinate institutionalized spirituality in a determinate material organization of relations between people."[16] Systemic evils manifest what Fleming Rutledge calls the "moral unintelligibility of evil" active as public policy.[17] The list of illustrations in the twentieth and twenty-first centuries is mind numbing. In the words of M. Scott Peck, systemic evil "masquerades as sane" and presents "destructiveness as normal."[18]

During the seminar on the Holocaust mentioned earlier, one guest speaker was an elderly Holocaust survivor who operated a shoe repair shop in South Kansas City. He sat before us and talked about life in a Nazi concentration

---

14. Ibid., 7.

15. Walter Wink, *Naming the Powers: The Language of Power in the New Testament* (Philadelphia: Fortress Press, 1984), 145.

16. Ibid., 109.

17. Rutledge, *Crucifixion*, 441-43.

18. M. Scott Peck, *The People of the Lie* (New York: Simon and Schuster, 1983), 265.

As humans we often contribute to and draw life from social systems alienated from God's purposes for creation. The fall cuts across everything that makes us human—sexuality and death, work and civilization, culture and ethics.

camp. We asked, "What did you do in the concentration camp?" Our guest reached into his coat pocket and pulled out a small plastic box. Once opened, the box revealed a shriveled bar of soap. Extending the box for us to see its contents, our guest said, "We made soap." Impressed on the soap, clearly visible in German, were the words *rein Juden fett* (pure Jewish fat). The "system" had put the imprisoned Jews to work making soap from the bodies of exterminated Jews. Many individuals who were operating death camps later said they were just fulfilling their assigned roles in the system. German philosopher Hannah Arendt was shocked by how mundane, how routine evil can be.[19]

New Testament scholars observe how competing social structures cooperated to crucify Jesus. The Sadducees and Pharisees conspired to use the complex Jewish religious system to bring about Jesus's death. The Gospels detail how the otherwise admirable Roman legal and governmental structure[20] was manipulated to make Jesus's crucifixion legal. Walter Wink observes that Jesus was crucified, not because he did something wrong, but because he violated the "system" of the "Powers"; he shook the "system" to its "invisible foundations." He had to be eliminated.[21]

As humans we often contribute to and draw life from social systems alienated from God's purposes for creation. The fall cuts across everything that makes us human—sexuality and death, work and civilization, culture and ethics. It manifests deadly fruit individually and structurally.

---

19. Hannah Arendt used the phrase "the banality of evil" to describe Adolf Eichmann, a major organizer of the Holocaust. See "Eichmann in Jerusalem Quotes," taken from Hannah Arendt, *Eichmann in Jerusalem: A Report on the Banality of Evil* (New York: Viking Press, 1963; New York: Penguin, 2006), Goodreads, https://www.goodreads.com/work/quotes/1023716-eichmann-in-jerusalem-a-report-on-the-banality-of-evil.

20. The apostle Paul, a Roman citizen, effectively used it to appeal his stalled legal process to the emperor himself (Acts 25:1-12).

21. Wink, *Naming the Powers*, 109.

The grace of God makes it both necessary and possible to confront the full range of the fall. To speak of "fall" attests that "the image of God," not sin, defines God's intention for us. Sin does not define what it means to be human. The victorious Christ and the indwelling Holy Spirit make it possible to address sin, no matter its form, by being continuously transformed (metamorphosed) in the image of Christ (2 Cor. 3:18; Rom. 8:29; Col 3:10). The risen Christ, not disobedient Adam, is this world's intended future.

"Person" for the Hebrews and Paul

The rise of modernity had numerous sources and profound consequences for our perception of reality (modernity comes in several versions, such as in Western Europe and Latin America). One result in Western societies was the rise of individualism.[22] Individualism is the belief that the individual is the most real unit of society. Associations or corporate entities are secondary. "Individualism is the idea that the fundamental unit of the human species that thinks, lives, and acts toward goals is the individual."[23] "The thread that has run through western civilization since the sixteenth century," observes sociologist Daniel Bell, "is that the social unit of society is not the group, the guild, the tribe, or the city but the person."[24] Individuals arbitrarily "create" corporate structures, not vice versa.

Sometimes individualism is referred to as the "atomization of society" because the social fabric is broken into smaller, "atomistic" parts. Though the individual is aware

22. This section is not meant to undercut the importance of the individual, but only to expose the harm of individualist excesses and as they relate to the church and human community.

23. Eric MacIntosh, "What Is Individualism? What Is Collectivism?" *Objectivism in Depth* (blog), January 22, 2016, https://objectivismindepth.com /2016/01/22/what-is-individualism-what-is-collectivism/.

24. Daniel Bell, *The Cultural Contradictions of Capitalism* (New York: Basic Books, 1996), 16.

of large social structures such as family, church, or state, the self remains conceptually intact and identifiable from the whole. Life's major value is self-fulfillment.

Individualism has undergone numerous modifications. But its fundamental meaning remains. The Western psyche is individualistic, not corporate. Sociologist Alexander Riley says individualism is "modernity's baseline force." It "burns away supportive webs of mutual dependence." It "works against the collective symbols, norms, and rites that have been the glue of human society from time immemorial." And it erodes any remaining sense of the sacred.[25] A hallmark of postmodernity is that there are "no metanarratives," no universal unifying "narrative" of meaning for all humankind. For example, there are many individual "moral narratives," but no universal moral norm.

Once individualism works its way into a culture's psyche, it becomes "reality," and one wonders how anyone could think otherwise. It is common for Westerners to speak of individual rights but difficult for them to think about social, corporate rights or well-being.

In cultures much less influenced by the seventeenth- and eighteenth-century European and North American Enlightenment, being part of a larger social whole is far more constitutive of personhood than it is in Western individualism.

Emergence of individualism had numerous sources. One was the decline of philosophical realism. Another was the European Wars of Religion following the Protestant Reformation.

In Europe, during most of the Middle Ages (roughly from the fall of Rome in 476 to the beginning of the fourteenth-century Renaissance), modern individualism was

---

25. Alexander Riley, "A Religion of Activism," *First Things* (April 2019): 9-11, https://www.firstthings.com/article/2019/04/a-religion-of-activism.

unheard of. A person knew himself to be "person" only as part of a more fundamental, universal social whole such as the church. The "universal" is most "real" (realism, closely associated with Plato's doctrine of forms).[26] The individual is a secondary "instance" of the "universal." The individual gained identity as part of a more fundamental "whole."[27]

In the fourteenth century the prominence of realism began to be replaced by the rise and eventual dominance of a philosophy known as "nominalism" (also known as *terminism* and *anti-realism*).

Nominalism is most closely associated with the English Franciscan William of Ockham (ca. 1287–1347), who taught that universals result from an act of the intellect (understanding) in which similar things are assigned a universal concept or sign or name such as "horse" or "man." No *universal reality* corresponds to the concept.[28] The individual thing is the most real. For example, when we group individual Christians, we need a name for them. So we call them "church," a *name* for individuals thought of as a whole. "Church" isn't a *primary reality* that *precedes* and *transcends* while *including* individual Christians. Rather, Christians "join" other Christians with whom they agree and provide community; they name it "church."

By contrast, for the apostle Paul, the church is Christ's body to which Christians are joined through the Holy Spirit (Rom. 12:4-5; 1 Cor. 12:27; Eph. 5:21-33; Col. 1:18). As created by Christ through the Spirit, the church precedes and

---

26. As was true for Thomas Aquinas (1225-74), the universal could be considered an "idea" (e.g., human) in the mind of God, not a "thing" in which all individual humans share.

27. Realism had its origin in many sources, two of which were the Greek philosophers Plato (ca. 424–ca. 348 BC) and Aristotle (ca. 384-ca. 322 BC). Belief in "universals" undergirded the Catholic belief that the "essence" of the bread and wine in the Eucharist could be distinguished from their material "accidents."

28. Similarities give rise to universal concepts. There is no metaphysical reason for the similarities except divine choice.

transcends believers while including them in *koinonia* (Gk., *koinōnia* [fellowship]) with the Father; they are members of Christ's visible body in the world. Our koinonia with one another is constituted by koinonia, *communion*, with Christ (cf. 1 John 1:3). We are *baptized* into his person, into his body, and share in him, and with each other, by the Spirit through the *proclaimed Word* and *Eucharist*. The mystery of the church should never be distorted to mean mere mutual interest, including doctrinal interest.

Paul was a Jew and a member of the larger Greco-Roman world. His psychology—that is, his perception of "person"—was strongly influenced by his Hebrew context, where "person" was understood holistically. Parts of the body have independent physical or psychical functions. But there is interdependence between each part, reliant upon the whole. Individual parts represent the whole and have no final identity apart from it.

This holistic understanding of the body carries over into the community and results in a "corporate" understanding of community. Just as in the body there is an interdependence of each part upon the whole, in the community an individual has meaning, receives identity, only as related to the group. Apart from the community there is no person.[29]

Paul's understanding of personhood was also shaped by his understanding of what it means to be "in Christ." New Testament scholar Ben Dunson has shown that for Paul the individual Christian, and the community (the church), are intricately intertwined; there is an essential connection between the individual and the community.[30]

---

29. Max E. Polley, "The Place of Henry Wheeler Robinson among Old Testament Scholars," *The Baptist Quarterly* 24, no. 6 (April 1972): 274, https://biblicalstudies.org.uk/pdf/bq/24-6_271.pdf.

30. Ben C. Dunson, *Individual and Community in Paul's Letter to the Romans* (Tübingen, DEU: Mohr Siebeck, 2012).

There are no "individual" Christians as we commonly perceive them. "Individual" and "community" must be understood together.

Clearly, by Paul's standard, modern individualism ill-equips us to comprehend the meaning and extent of redemption, as well as the relationship between the individual and the body of Christ (koinonia). Individualism also leaves us poorly equipped to understand sin as more than individual acts of volition. For Paul, evil is not only individual but also systemic and corporate (Eph. 6:12-13). His understanding of personhood and the "not yet" of our redemption prepares us to recognize and confront our involvement in powers that continue to oppose the kingdom of God. His understanding of the "hope" that awaits us at the kingdom's consummation equips us as the body of Christ, by grace, to recognize the reality of corporate evil, to confess its impact upon us, and in the power of the risen Christ to confront it.

Paul and the Powers

The language of power pervades the New Testament. The term introduces a complex matrix of related terms and concepts that, but for the aid of scholars, would leave us confused and wondering what the language has to do with Christian discipleship in the twenty-first century. Some, not waiting for scholarly assistance, launch into the language on their own. They generate a mythic world of demons and angelic powers unrelated to Jesus Christ, who is Lord of the powers. Their speculations usually ignore the church's mission of making known to "the principalities and powers in heavenly places . . . the manifold wisdom of God" (Eph. 3:10, KJV; cf. 1 Cor. 3:9).

Paul understands the powers, primarily as they relate to earthly structures in which the powers are manifest. For him, the powers are earthly and cosmic, good and evil, human (including structures) and demonic, individual and corporate. David Watson says that "Paul's intention in using these various terms is to indicate the profusion and power of the spiritual agents exerting themselves upon human lives. His speech is aggregate, piling one term upon another for emphasis."[31] Paul's intention is not to give a detailed inventory of the powers that inhabit the heavens, but to notify the church of the multiplicity of demonic forces allied against it.[32] G. B. Caird said the powers frequently "act in defiance of God's purpose and to the enslavement of mankind. They stand, as their names imply, for political, social, economic and religious structures of power."[33]

According to Paul, on the cross, Christ "disarmed" the enslaving powers and "triumph[ed] over them" (Col. 2:15). We will concentrate on the powers, not in their isolated form as spiritual beings or demonic forces, but in their historical embodiment as they abduct and employ for the purpose of human enslavement otherwise legitimate structures.

The primary Pauline term for power is the Greek word *exousia* (pl. *exousiai*). Most often *exousia* (85 percent of the time) refers to structural dimensions of earthly existence, established by some authorizing person or body. The battery of terms associated with *exousia* mean essentially the same thing. Their meanings depend on the context in which they are used. The language is imprecise and interchangeable. One or more terms can represent the whole. Apparently his original readers were sufficiently conversant with the terms and understood them in context.

Nine times Paul uses diverse terms to speak of the powers: Romans 8:38-39 ("principalities" and "powers"); 1

---

31. David Watson, "The Ontology of Principalities and Powers," *Wesleyan Theological Journal* 56, no. 1 (Spring 2021): 53.

32. Ibid.

33. Caird, *Language and Imagery of the Bible*, 242.

Corinthians 2:8 ("rulers of this age");[34] 15:24-26 ("authority and power"); Ephesians 1:20-21 ("rule and authority and power and dominion and . . . name"); 2:2 ("the prince of the power of the air"); 3:10 ("principalities and powers in the heavenly places"); 6:12 ("principalities," "powers," "world rulers," and "spiritual hosts of wickedness"); Colossians 1:16 ("thrones," "dominions," "principalities," and "authorities"); 2:15 ("principalities and powers").[35]

Whatever the terms being used, the powers have violated God's will by enslaving legitimate human structures and the persons who populate them. As subverted and possessed, structures acquire the characteristics—a "spirit"—of a "transcendent" evil force or power. They are "spiritual" as "embodied."[36] Christians do not "wrestle against" structures *as such*, but against their systemic distortion and their fierce opposition to God's holy reign. Like any other part of God's creation, otherwise legitimate structures are impacted by the fall and become forms of bondage from which Christ must set us free.

Structures impacted by the powers correspond approximately to what we earlier labeled "orders of creation."[37] They give unity and direction to life.[38] They are the "weight-bearing substratum of the world," the "underpinnings of creation."[39] They are not "mere accidents of history or human

---

34. In 1 Cor. 2:7-8 Paul says that if "the rulers of this age" had known the "hidden wisdom of God," they "would not have crucified the Lord of glory." See Walter Wink's discussion of the powers as being ignorant of God's plan. Wink, *Naming the Powers*, 113-18.

35. Three times (Gal. 4:3, 9; Col. 2:8) Paul refers to *stoikeia*, "elements." The term cannot be reduced to a single meaning but must be understood in context. In Galatians *stoikeia* probably refers to the "gods" of the Galatians' pagan past.

36. Wink, *Naming the Powers*, 105.

37. Berkhof, *Christ and the Powers*, 29.

38. Ibid., 32-33.

39. Ibid., 28-29.

fabrications."[40] Rather, in and through them (e.g., the family) we achieve human meaning. They form "the linkage between God's love and visible human experience." Berkhof says they are "the dikes [by] which God encircles His good creation, to keep it in His fellowship and protect it from chaos."[41] They "hold life together, preserving it within God's love, serving as aids to bind men fast in His fellowship."[42] Structures are "the good creations of a good God," negatively affected by the fall and *often* abducted for Satan's use.[43]

Meant to give unity and direction to life, as impacted by evil, "orders of creation" are bent toward claiming ultimate meaning for the world and human life.[44] As *corrupted* they become "gods" (Gal. 4:8). Even the law, the temple, and religion can become idols, demanding ultimate allegiance, worship (Rev. 13:1-18). "This is the demonic reversal which has taken place on the invisible side of creation. No longer do the Powers bind man and God together; they separate them. They stand as a road-block between the Creator and His creation."[45] As the "rulers of this age" (1 Cor. 2:6), they are in conflict with the Lord of Glory. As fallen, morality, fixed religious and ethical rules, the administration of justice, and the ordering of the state exercise tyranny over human life.

The New Testament affirms civil political structures created for justly governing human relationships. But it also challenges the growing cult of emperor worship, particularly prominent in the eastern part of the Roman Empire.

---

40. Wink, *Naming the Powers*, 50. "They have their place in the created order. They suffer all the consequences of the fall." Even then they "cannot separate believers from the love of God because they cannot even separate themselves" from God's love (50).

41. Berkhof, *Christ and the Powers*, 29.

42. Ibid., 29.

43. Wink, *Naming the Powers*, 104.

44. Berkhof, *Christ and the Powers*, 32-33.

45. Ibid., 30.

Rather than call Caesar "Lord" (*Kyrios*), early Christians affirmed, "God has made this Jesus, whom you crucified, both Lord and Messiah" (Acts 2:36, NIV). Today, as always, Christians are being challenged by "empire," urged to assign the title *Kyrios* to ideologies in many forms.

Paul had learned from Christ that the risen Lord, not the powers, rules the world. "When Jesus was crucified and rose from the dead, and since then wherever this saving event is proclaimed, the domination of the world powers is at an end" (see Col. 1:15-17). This proclamation is central to everything Paul says about the powers (2:13-15).[46] On the cross, Jesus achieved release of sinners from guilt and from slavery to the powers.[47] Previously they were treated as the fundamental and ultimate realities. They were the "god[s] of this world" (2 Cor. 4:4). Now that the true God has been revealed in Jesus Christ, it is "apparent that the Powers are inimical to him, acting not as his instruments, but as his adversaries."[48]

Paul's language may appear abstract and ancient. When Westerners hear him speaking about the powers that threatened Christian discipleship in his day, we can too easily file it away as something applicable to his context, but not to ours. It sounds too mythical for persons who no longer live in the Greco-Roman world inhabited by threatening cosmic powers. And besides, we might say, the comprehensive empire system the Romans hurled against Christ and the church no longer exists. However, today Christians in many world regions do face martyrdom.[49]

---

46. Ibid., 36.

47. Ibid., 37.

48. Ibid., 38.

49. The 2019 "World Watch List" of Open Doors USA identified fifty countries where it is most dangerous to follow Jesus—from North Korea to Azerbaijan. "The World Watch List," OpenDoorsUSA.org/WWL.

The powers as Paul described them have no temporal, religious, cultural, political, or economic limitations. Mature Christian discipleship requires detecting them, recognizing their impact upon us, and discerning our participation in them as much today as in Paul's day. An understanding of sin, salvation, the power of the risen Christ, and growth in his image that dismisses this part of the New Testament gravely mispresents the gospel, the urgency of honesty and confession, and the magnitude of what Christ's victory must address, in us and in the world.

If Paul were here, he might begin by asking us to examine where companies that manage our retirement accounts invest their/our funds. Are we reaping long-term benefits from alcohol and entertainment industries that contribute to human degradation?

Even when contemporary Christians attempt to steer clear of the powers, they can be betrayed. To steer clear of morally questionable investments, many Christians invest "ethically" by choosing "socially responsible" mutual funds. In a September 1, 2018, *Wall Street Journal* article, Jon Sindreu and Sarah Kent showed that "with little regulation governing what a fund manager can call a 'socially responsible' or 'ethical' investment," increasingly many fund strategies are "designed to beat the market rather than uphold morality." A "dizzying array" of mutual fund possibilities has been created. "Fund companies can craft their definitions in such a way that they simply rename existing products with an ethical illusion, without having to change . . . fund holdings." Fund managers have rebranded at least two dozen existing mutual funds over the past few years. They use new names such as "sustainable" and "ESG" (environmental, social, and corporate governance). The fund managers conceal the truth about how "morally sensitive" funds are being invested. The ethical investment industry has learned that "shunning sin" stocks hamper investment returns. "So, with the priority on returns rather than ethics, fewer stocks are excluded outright."[50]

Contemporary illustrations of the presence and influence of "the powers" could extend almost endlessly. They could include Norman Wirzba's wrenching description of the devastating impact upon the land in Appalachia caused by mountaintop-removal (MTR) mining. MTR is used to extract coal. It blows up entire mountains that gradually disappear, while valleys slowly fill and ecosystems vanish. "The damage inflicted upon the land and wildlife of Appalachia," Wirzba observes, "cannot be neatly separated from the damage inflicted upon its people."[51]

Much closer to home, although workers in Asian sweatshops are being replaced by automation (creating a new set of problems), many of us have purchased branded apparel without giving a thought to the working conditions that made our purchases affordable. And let us be reminded that "deals" from China, we so hungrily purchase, are produced in a country ruled by a totalitarian Communist government that as of 2019 had imprisoned hundreds of thousands of Uighur Muslims in "reeducation" camps with the sole purpose of destroying their religious minority. With increasing frequency churches, mosques, and Tibetan Buddhist schools are being destroyed, while China tells the world of its support for religious freedom.[52]

These illustrations should alert us to the fact that when Paul speaks of "contending" against "powers" and "principalities" (Eph. 6:12), we are included. The battle occurs *in* and *around* us as Christians. As Eric R. Severson persua-

50. Jon Sindreu and Sarah Kent, "Why It's So Hard to Be an 'Ethical' Investor," *Wall Street Journal*, September 1, 2018.

51. Wirzba, *Way of Love*, 140.

52. Thomas F. Farr, "Diplomacy and Persecution in China," *First Things* (May 2019): 29-35, https://www.firstthings.com/article/2019/05/diplomacy-and-persecution-in-china.

sively and extensively explains in *Scandalous Obligation*, the gospel of the kingdom of God makes it both necessary and possible to recognize and confront the powers wherever and in whatever form they appear.[53] The love of God calls us to "unmask" the powers in ourselves and in our world. "The healing of a wounded world," says Wirzba, "is the heart of the good-news life that Christians are called to live. . . . The primary task is to put the love of God to work in the world. Church is the place where Christians learn to . . . practice the skills of nurture, healing, and reconciliation. They learn to swim in the flow of God's love, so they can channel and apply that love wherever they might be."[54]

The New Testament leaves no doubt. Subverted and distorted "powers" must be subjected to the crucified and risen Christ. Paul tells the Corinthian Christians that "[Christ] must reign until he has put all his enemies under his feet. The last enemy to be destroyed is death" (1 Cor. 15:25-26). The battle will continue until total triumph becomes a reality on all fronts, and visible to all (v. 24). *That is future.* He tells the Christians in Colossae that on the cross (the pivot of history), contrary to what the world observed, Christ "disarmed the powers and authorities, he made a public spectacle of them, triumphing over them by the cross" (2:15, NIV; John 12:31). The claims for deity from which they had gained authority have been struck from their hands. Their alleged authority over us was an illusion. Their ability to deceive has been stripped.[55] *That is past.* Christ *is* Lord and *will be* Lord over all.[56]

---

53. Eric R. Severson, *Scandalous Obligation: Rethinking Christian Responsibility* (Kansas City: Beacon Hill Press, 2011), 85-98.

54. Wirzba, *Way of Love*, 166.

55. Berkhof, *Christ and the Powers*, 39.

56. Wink, *Naming the Powers*, 60-61.

But this does not mean "that with one blow their ungodly working has been put to a stop."[57] The tyrannical spiritual powers are now being defeated by those who "will no longer let themselves be enslaved, led astray, and intimidated."[58] "Already" the powers have been robbed of their power to force a defection from Christ (Rom. 8:31-39). We are living in the power of the "already" and, by the Spirit, living toward the "not yet." "The hurricane of new creation," N. T. Wright says of the liberating gospel Paul preached, can't be put "back into the bottle of the old world."[59] Ultimate victory is certain (1 Cor. 15:24-26).[60]

When Paul lists the gifts of the Spirit in 1 Corinthians 12:8-10, he names the "discernment of spirits." This includes discerning the powers which "hold the hearts and actions of men under their sway in specific times and places."[61] "Where the victorious kingship of Christ is confessed," says Berkhof, "there prevails a consistent unbelief" in the boast of the powers.[62] When created powers become idolatrous and demonic, "the church's task is to unmask this idolatry and recall the Powers to their created purposes in the world." Through the church they must "learn how comprehensive God's wisdom really is."[63]

Conclusion

For a theology justifiably to claim fidelity to the New Testament and human experience, it must make ample

---

57. Berkhof, *Christ and the Powers*, 39.

58. Ibid., 44.

59. Wright, *Paul: A Biography*, 158.

60. Paul was conscious of living in the opening scenes of the new drama of world history, with heaven and earth now held together not by Torah and temple but by Jesus and the Spirit, pointing forward to the time when the divine glory would fill the world and transform it from top to bottom. Ibid., 405.

61. Berkhof, *Christ and the Powers*, 47.

62. Ibid., 49.

63. Wink, *Naming the Powers*, 4.

space for the powers in its doctrines of sin and salvation. The form of Christian piety and liturgy it fosters must do the same. It will bid the Holy Spirit to continue exposing places in our lives, our cultures, and our churches where the powers are operative and have not been unmasked, disarmed, and redeemed.[64] Being shaped, sanctified (1 Thess. 5:23-24), in the image of Christ requires throwing our lives wide open to our "disarming" Lord. Grace and love make this possible and necessary. It will continue as part of Christian piety until the "perishable" puts on the "imperishable" at the day of the Lord (1 Cor. 15:53). In the meantime, as Paul testified of himself (Phil. 3:12-16), in the Spirit's power we should be steadily transforming more "not yet" into more "already"—a continual conversion (Rom. 16:25-27; Eph. 6:12; Phil. 3:12-16).

Without diminishing the importance of the powers, it is more important to remember they no longer have the final word.

N. T. Wright reminds us that because of Jesus's crucifixion the dark powers were disarmed (Col. 2:13-15). They can still protest and vent their furor. But Jesus's power is greater—the power of forgiveness. A new creation has been inaugurated. The past has been erased and a revolution, a new world, has been initiated, one in which power now means the power of love. Good news! This world now has a new Lord![65] In this spirit, Walter Wink urges Christians in each concrete situation to rediscover what it means for Christ to be sovereign over the powers.[66]

---

64. "Fidelity to the gospel," says Walter Wink, "lies not in repeating its slogans but in plunging the prevailing idolatries into its corrosive acids." Ibid., 111, 115.

65. Wright, *Day the Revolution Began*, 391.

66. Wink, *Naming the Powers*, 148.

Yea, Amen! Let all adore Thee,
　High on Thy eternal throne;
Savior, take the pow'r and glory,
　Claim the kingdom for Thine own.
Hallelujah! Hallelujah!
　Everlasting God, come down![67]

---

67. Charles Wesley, "Lo! He Comes, with Clouds Descending," in *Wesley Hymns* (Kansas City: Lillenas, 1982), no. 11.

NINE

Christus Victor?

Alleluia, alleluia, alleluia!
The strife is o'er, the battle done;
the victory of life is won;
the song of triumph has begun.
Alleluia![1]

One *either* believes *or* does not believe that on the cross of Jesus Christ, and in his resurrection, the creator, covenant-maker, and covenant-keeper God dealt mightily and decisively with sin. Jesus as *Christus Victor either* did *or* did not successfully disarm "the principalities and powers" so that we who were "dead in trespasses" might be "made alive together with him" (Col. 2:13-15). The New Testament offers no middle ground. If one believes and is possessed by the former, and if one loves the God who in Christ defeated death, hell, sin, and the grave, there is nothing left to do but, by the power of the Holy Spirit, give oneself without reservation to him, to his purposes, to his kingdom, and to his reconciling, transforming, and sanctifying grace.

Even a murderer named "the Misfit," in Flannery O'Connor's "A Good Man Is Hard to Find," agreed. "If [Jesus]

---

1. Anonymous seventeenth-century Latin hymn, "The Strife Is O'er, the Battle Done," trans. Francis Pott (1861), Hymnary.org, https://hymnary.org/text /the_strife_is_oer_the_battle_done.

did what He said, then it's nothing for you to do but throw away everything and follow Him, and if He didn't, then it's nothing for you to do but enjoy the few minutes you got left the best way you can."[2] Dietrich Bonhoeffer knew it: "When Christ calls a man, he bids him come and die."[3]

How the provisions of *Christ the Victor* are to be appropriated, and how they are to be demonstrated in life, may differ from one theological tradition to another. But the Christological center and provision must not. New Testament scholar Luke Timothy Johnson says, "The real Jesus is the one who is now alive and powerfully present, through the Holy Spirit, in the lives of human beings."[4]

If a Christian believes sin and its offspring continue functionally to be God's equal, the best he or she can expect from the Holy Spirit is marginal success in combating the flesh. With integrity, that person should then abandon the Christian faith as a failure. He or she should either move to some other "solution" or perhaps abandon religion altogether. If Christ accomplished no more than some theologies describe, then calling him *Christus Victor* is farcical and unworthy of support.

If unending struggle with sin's dark power rather than "new creation" that "transforms a person from the inside out"[5] had been Paul's missionary message, it would never have penetrated the Greco-Roman world. From city to city, to those once bound by idolatry, he proclaimed that the same "incomparably great power" by which God raised Jesus from the dead was now being unleashed in those

---

2. Flannery O'Connor, "A Good Man Is Hard to Find," in *Flannery O'Connor: The Complete Stories* (New York: Farrar, Straus and Giroux, 1971), 132.

3. Dietrich Bonhoeffer, *The Cost of Discipleship* (New York: Touchstone Book, 1995), 87.

4. Luke Timothy Johnson, *The Real Jesus* (San Francisco: HarperSanFrancisco, 1996), 144.

5. Wright, *Paul: A Biography*, 406.

who believe (Eph. 1:18-20, NIV). And if the apostles had not believed that in Jesus Messiah, promise of a new covenant (Jer. 31:31-35) had been fulfilled and that through the Spirit, its provisions had become internalized and lived out among God's new covenant people, they certainly would not have given their lives for its proclamation.

If the work of Jesus Christ on the cross achieved no more than a lifelong struggle between being willing to do "what is right" but being unable because of the "sin which dwells in me" (Rom. 7:15-20), God should apologize to the martyrs. Did they die in defense of a pitiful Jesus who tried his best but did not accomplish very much?

Theologies that defend marginality over against Christian holiness should either be declared superior to a wealth of contemporary New Testament scholarship or put in practice the *sola Scriptura* they so repeatedly assert. It is too late to edit the New Testament to suit theological preferences for restricted discipleship, and it is indefensible to inhabit doctrinal silos.

To say that expecting more than a perpetual struggle against indwelling sin will inevitably lead to self-righteousness, infringement of *grace alone*, and indefensible perfectionism is a "red herring" now worn to the bone. Contemporary New Testament scholarship has exploded that fallacy.

For others, there is a strange belief that if Christians make the transforming power of God, as described in Romans 8, the norm for Christian life, this somehow diminishes the doctrine of justification by grace through faith alone. Somehow, for them, radical transformation from the inside out that makes "living according to the Spirit" (v. 5) the Christian norm elevates human accomplishment at the expense of grace and faith. Supposedly, recognizing an unconquerable law of the flesh that continues to characterize Christians prompts them toward a radical dependence upon grace.

For example, Martin Luther, in his commentary on Paul's epistle to the Galatians, said, "Paradoxically, a Christian is both right and wrong, holy and profane, an enemy of God and a child of God. These contradictions no person can harmonize who does not understand the true way of salvation."[6] Luther observes that

> Christian righteousness is the confidence of the heart in God through Christ Jesus. Such confidence is accounted righteousness for Christ's sake. Two things make for Christian righteousness: Faith in Christ, which is a gift of God; and God's acceptance of this imperfect faith of ours for perfect righteousness. Because of my faith in Christ, God overlooks my distrust, the unwillingness of my spirit, my many other sins. Because the shadow of Christ's wing covers me I have no fear [but] that God will cover all my sins and take my imperfections for perfect righteousness.
>
> God "winks" at my sins. . . . God says: "Because you believe in My Son I will forgive your sins until death shall deliver you from the body of sin."[7]

According to Luther, Christians remain sinners wholly deserving the judgment of God while also being "accounted" righteous by the righteousness of Christ. Luther used the Latin phrase *simul iustus et peccator* to articulate his doctrine. The phrase means "simultaneously righteous and sinner." Methodist theologian Geoffrey Wainwright says that for some Lutheran theologians *simul iustus et peccator*

---

6. Martin Luther, *A Commentary on St. Paul's Epistle to the Galatians*, 1535, trans. Theodore Graebner (Grand Rapids: Zondervan, 1949), comm. on Gal. 3:6, CCEL, https://www.ccel.org/ccel/luther/galatians.pdf.

7. Ibid.

meant "the believer became one hundred per cent justified while remaining one hundred percent sinner."[8]

Lutheran theologian Craig Nessan calls the doctrine of sanctification "the Lutheran 'Achilles Heel.'" "Understanding the relationship between justification and sanctification became and remains a challenge."[9] There have been numerous efforts to show that when Luther is correctly understood, sanctification lies at the heart of his theology. A major contemporary effort is under way by the Finnish School under the leadership of Tuomo Mannermaa and his students. The Finnish School teaches that official *Lutheran* doctrine is quite different from Luther's own theology. The distinction between justification and sanctification, they contend, is foreign to Luther's thought. Correctly understood, Luther believed that "the doctrine of justification . . . is a matter of Christ abiding in the heart of the believer." "Theosis [sanctification], rather than being a foreign Orthodox concept, is in fact one of the images Luther used to describe salvation."[10]

The substance of Luther's *simul iustus et peccator,* if not its exact form, has passed into much of Protestant theology and practice. Many believe the best a Christian can hope for in this life is for God to "cover our sins by Christ's righteousness." Christians continue to be at once both enemies *and* children of God.

John Calvin did not speak of Christians as God's "enemies." But he believed that although a person is "al-

---

8. Wainwright, *Doxology,* 132.

9. Craig L. Nessan, "The Relation of Justification and Sanctification in the Lutheran Tradition," ch. 5 in *All Things Needed for Godliness: A Portrait of Holiness among Christian Traditions* (Kansas City: Foundry Publishing, 2020), 84.

10. Veli-Matti Kärkkäinen, *One with God: Salvation as Deification and Justification* (Collegeville, MN: Liturgical Press, 2004), 37-38. The Finnish School of Mannermaa argues that official Lutheran doctrine was shaped more by Philip Melanchthon (1497–1560), chief defender and interpreter of Luther, than by Luther himself.

Holiness of heart and life as provided for and designed by God Incarnate is normative Christian existence, not a dream to be deferred in deference to the power of sin.

ready regenerated" and is being "led to good by the Spirit of God," the "corruption of nature" continues to appear in him "conspicuously." As long as a Christian lives, corruption will "obstinately resist and lead to what is contrary" to God's will. The roiling conflict about which Paul speaks in Romans 7:14-24 "does not exist in man [until] he is renewed by the Spirit of God."[11]

Whether the power of the Holy Spirit unleashed in a believer can produce victorious Christian living is not to be settled by Augustine, Luther, Calvin, Wesley, or any other theologian. It was decisively answered on Calvary, by Jesus's resurrection and by Pentecostal power. Easter faith affirms that to be "in" Christ by the Holy Spirit involves being daily transformed by him, daily formed in his image, becoming more and more godly by grace through faith alone.

Through the power of the Holy Spirit, the risen Christ provides a holy life for believers. For his people he has indeed "disarmed the principalities and powers and made a public example of them, triumphing over them in him" (Col. 2:15). He has delivered his people from the kingdom of darkness and transferred them into his kingdom (1:13). Holiness of heart and life as provided for and designed by God Incarnate is normative Christian existence, not a dream to be deferred in deference to the power of sin.

We live in an era of superb biblical scholarship that makes continuing many of our old theological disputes sound like defending a "flat earth." Whether one is Eastern Orthodox, Roman Catholic, Reformed, Anglican, Wesleyan, or Pentecostal, the time has come to allow our theologies to be informed by current biblical scholarship. A primary paradigm shift seems to have happened, prompted in part by a restoration of the gospel as the good news of the long-awaited, now-inaugurated kingdom of God and the launching of

---

11. Calvin, *Commentary on Romans*, comm. on Rom. 7:15.

new creation here on earth; the implications of calling Jesus *Kyrios* (Lord) in the Greco-Roman world; and the challenge to *empire* posed by the risen Christ, who is Lord of all. It is indefensible to retain historically conditioned theologies if that entails ignoring what the Spirit is saying to the church through current advances in biblical studies. "The canonical Scriptures," Lutheran theologian Peter Brunner said, with their "concrete authority," must be free to exercise "their office of judge over all teachers and doctrine in the Church." "Through the work of the Holy Ghost," let the "harmonious voices of the Scriptural witnesses" be heard in the church as "the saving word of the Gospel."[12]

Today the call to vital Christian holiness as informed by the fruit of current biblical studies spans historic divisions in the church.

George Weigel: Baptized into Holiness

George Weigel, a prominent American Catholic intellectual, says, "In its *Dogmatic Constitution on the Church* the Second Vatican Council [1962-65] spoke eloquently about the universality of the call to holiness.[13] The Lord himself, the Council Fathers recalled, 'preached holiness of life . . . to each and every one of his disciples without distinction . . . : 'You, therefore, must be perfect, as your heavenly Father is perfect' [Matt. 5:48]."[14]

---

12. Peter Brunner, "Commitment to the Lutheran Confession: What Does It Mean Today?" *The Springfielder* 33, no. 3 (December 1969): 5, http://www.ctsfw.net/media/pdfs/brunnercommitmenttoconfessions.pdf.

13. Chapter 5 of *Lumen Gentium* (Light of the Nations) is titled "The Universal Call to Holiness in the Church." *Lumen Gentium* systematically defines the Dogmatic Constitution on the Church. It is the second of four defining documents of the Second Vatican Council. Paul VI, *Lumen Gentium*, Vatican Website, November 21, 1964, http://www.vatican.va/archive/hist_councils/ii_vatican_council/documents/vat-ii_const_19641121_lumen-gentium_en.html.

14. George Weigel, *Evangelical Catholicism: Deep Reform in the 21st-Century Church* (New York: Basic Books, 2013), 257. The statement is located in chapter 5, sec. 40 of *Lumen Gentium* (Light of the Nations). It is followed by these words:

"The first task of Evangelical Catholicism," Weigel says, "is to foster the holiness of all the people of the Church. That task, in turn, leads directly to mission." Moreover, the acceptance of evangelical responsibility is itself a means of sanctification, because "the Church's missionary spirituality is a journey toward holiness."[15]

But the temptation, Weigel warns, is to avoid the call to holiness and mission by "keeping a safe distance from the Lord Jesus." This is "a way of hedging our bets, of being 'reasonable' about our discipleship, of not looking too fanatical about this business of faith."[16] "But if you follow me," Jesus said, "you will find the holiness that is your heart's deepest desire. 'Follow me,' and be sent into mission."[17]

Christians, Weigel says, are "baptized into sanctity." They are "instructed by St. Paul to live 'as is fitting among saints' [Eph. 5:3] and to grow, 'as God's chosen ones, holy and beloved, [into] compassion, kindness, lowliness, meekness, and patience' [Col. 3:12]." Holiness, Weigel, insists, "is not an option for those who take baptism seriously. Holiness is an obligation, to be pursued not 'at a distance,' but through an ever-closer embrace of 'the Lamb of God, who takes away the sin[s] of the world' [John 1:29]."[18]

Weigel concludes his appeal for "deep reform in the Catholic Church" in arresting terms that know no denominational boundaries: "All true reform in the Church of the twenty-first century and beyond is thus ordered to holiness and mission. The Church is *semper reformanda*, always in

---

"The classes and duties of life are many, but holiness is one—that sanctity which is cultivated by all who are moved by the Spirit of God, and who obey the voice of the Father and worship God the Father in spirit and in truth." Paul VI, *Lumen Gentium*, ch. 5, sec. 41.

15. Weigel, *Evangelical Catholicism*, 258.
16. Ibid., 257.
17. Ibid.
18. Ibid., 257-58.

need of reform, 'not [to] be conformed to this world' [Rom. 12:2], but to be purified in holiness for mission."[19]

Let's learn from three scholars who are leading the way toward major restatements of the Christ's provisions for lives transformed by Christ through the Spirit's power.

N. T. Wright: A "Gospel-Driven Holiness"

In *The Day the Revolution Began*, New Testament scholar N. T. Wright says that a "real revolution" happened on the cross. Easter is its first sign. Because of Jesus's victory, the once-powerful world sovereigns have been forced to surrender their hold on humans. The idols have been dethroned.[20] Because of Jesus's victory, his disciples are to go out into the world armed with the power of the Holy Spirit. They are to proclaim that a new reality has arrived. Its name is God's forgiveness. It can be obtained by repenting and forsaking idolatry. This new kind of power "is the chain-breaking, idol-smashing, sin-abandoning power called 'forgiveness,' called 'utter gracious love,' called *Jesus*."[21]

A gospel-defined and "gospel-driven holiness" is required for the Messiah's crucified, resurrected, and new-creation people. This is what it means to be "new-Passover people" who accept their new-covenant vocation.[22]

To ignore or deny the mandatory "gospel-driven holiness" declared by Paul is to act as though the rulers of the "present evil age" (1:4) still rule the world. It is to conduct one's life as though the ultimate revelation of God's love and power has not happened. Too many Christians paddle around in the shallows when not far away awaits the marvelous and risky ocean of the gospel. It calls believers to

---

19. Ibid., 259.
20. Wright, *Day the Revolution Began*, 323.
21. Ibid., 384.
22. Ibid., 244-45.

plunge in. Permit the waves of God's glory to wash over us, cleanse us completely, and deliver us to the land of God's new creation.[23]

Fleming Rutledge:
A New Adam and a New Humanity

According to the gospel Paul preached, Fleming Rutledge says that God has by his mighty action in Christ, by the Spirit, created a new humanity, a new Adam. Through the Holy Spirit, he has bestowed his righteousness by which we are to conduct our lives.[24] It is true that a baptized Christian has no righteousness of his or her own. But God's righteousness is already ours because we are "in Christ."[25] Christians have been "incorporated into Christ by grace through faith."[26]

For Paul, recapitulation means Christians becoming what they already are. "Do not yield your members to sin as instruments of wickedness, but yield yourselves to God as men who have been brought from death to life, and your members to God as instruments of righteousness. For sin will have no dominion [will not lord it] over you, since you are not under law but under grace" (Rom. 6:13-14).

For Paul, being in Christ means being transferred from the old *kyrios* (sin) to the true *Kyrios*. To live by grace signifies that Christians have been "transferred" (Col. 1:13) from the kingdom of sin and death to the "kingdom of God's beloved Son" (v. 13). He is the one true *Kyrios*. In his kingdom no other *kyrios* can exercise lordship. Every part

---

23. Ibid., 415-16.

24. Rutledge, *Crucifixion*, 554.

25. Ibid. Rutledge notes that the phrase "in Christ" is used about forty times in Paul's undisputed letters.

26. Ibid.

of who we are has through baptism been transformed from death to life (Rom. 6:1-4).[27]

Michael J. Gorman:
Holiness as Cruciform Theosis

New Testament scholar Michael J. Gorman is representative of the rich advances in New Testament studies. In *Inhabiting the Cruciform God: Kenosis, Justification, and Theosis in Paul's Narrative Soteriology*, Gorman shows that for the apostle Paul, the faith that justifies is necessarily "both participatory and transforming."[28] It is first a participatory crucifixion while at the same time being life giving (cf. 2 Cor. 4:7-15). When a person exercises faith, and is crucified with Christ, he or she is resurrected while also remaining crucified.[29] The self is thereby "de-centered" and "re-centered" by and in Christ. Crucifixion is continuous.[30]

Justification by grace through faith means being drawn into Christ's self-emptying, his kenosis. It entails sharing in Christ's loving death. The result is continually participating in Christ. In Paul, there is a coordination between being made right or declared just before God (juridical), and participatory "baptism into Christ (e.g. Rom. 5–8)."[31] This is "cruciform faith," enabled by the Holy Spirit, who makes possible our participation in the faithful and loving death of Jesus, and also in his "resurrection life."[32]

"Justification by faith apart from works means justification by *grace-enabled participatory response*."[33] God's loving faithfulness as demonstrated in Christ's loving faithfulness

---

27. Ibid., 555.
28. Gorman, *Inhabiting the Crucified God*, 68.
29. Ibid., 70.
30. Ibid.
31. Ibid., 83.
32. Ibid., 84.
33. Ibid., 81.

is the means for our justification. Enabled by the Holy Spirit, we respond in faithfulness. Our faithfulness is expressed in love and co-crucifixion.[34] Justification is an action completely initiated by God. The Holy Spirit "effects" the experience of co-crucifixion and co-resurrection.[35] Faith means a complete, obedient response to the gospel (Rom. 1:5; 16:26). It entails thorough identification with our Lord's act of faithfulness and love.[36] It is "co-crucifixion."[37]

Gorman's explanation of cruciform faith sets the stage for his discussion of how Paul understands Christian holiness. He offers three pieces of evidence for saying Paul is "preoccupied with holiness." *First* is his use of *hagioi* ("holy ones"; sing., *hagios*) to address believers (Rom. 1:7; 1 Cor. 1:2; 2 Cor. 1:1; Phil. 1:1), and in twenty other instances. Paul gives particular attention to the church's holiness. Holiness is essential to the church's identity. *Second*, in openings to two letters, Paul uses *hagioi* to refer to God's calling. Believers are called to be holy ones (Rom. 1:7). Paul identifies the "church of God which is at Corinth" as those who have already been made holy and are "called to be saints [holy ones]" (1 Cor. 1:2). Holiness is the mandate and the goal (*telos*). It is both gift and task. The shape and substance of holiness are found "in Christ." *Third*, in Paul's letters, holiness appears as "programmatic statements." In 1 Thessalonians, for example, holiness is the most important theme, the essential will of God. Christian holiness means experiencing the triune God. Paul's basic message to the Thessalonians is a call to holiness (3:13; 5:23). "Holiness is also the focus of 1 Corinthians." In Romans, Paul claims that justification/reconciliation sets people free from idolatry and immorality. This is the work of God's love

---

34. Ibid.
35. Ibid., 69.
36. Ibid., 80.
37. Ibid., 79.

made known and effective through the Holy Spirit (5:1-11). Crucified and co-resurrected with Christ, believers offer themselves to God. As his servants, they serve God in a life of holiness (6:1-23). In Romans, conformity to the image of Christ (8:29), "rather than conformity to this age (12:1-2)," is the goal, the *telos*, of salvation.[38]

Christian holiness as theosis is not, for Paul, added to the gospel of God; it is gospel, good news. It means participating in Christ by God's enabling grace.[39] Christian holiness is the actualization of justification. It is Christlikeness.[40] It entails sharing in God's holiness brought to fruition by the Holy Spirit.[41] It is "covenant relationship with God; empowered by the Holy Spirit to live in Christlike, cruciform loyalty to God and love" for others.[42]

Grounded in the cross, Paul's gospel of holiness reveals three interrelated realities: "(1) the narrative identity of Christ the Son; (2) the essential character of God the Father; and (3) the primary activity of the Spirit."[43] Paul's experience of Son, Father, and Spirit resulted in a major reformulation of holiness as a counterintuitive imperative and a requisite communal process. Gorman summarizes Paul's doctrine of Christian holiness as a restatement of Leviticus 11:44-45; 19:2: "You shall be cruciform, for I am cruciform."[44]

Conclusion

The New Testament definitively and joyfully proclaims *Christus Victor*, who "has appeared once for all at the cul-

38. Ibid., 107-11.
39. Ibid., 110.
40. Ibid., 111.
41. Ibid., 112.
42. Gorman, *Death of the Messiah*, 45.
43. Ibid.
44. Ibid.

mination of the ages to do away with sin by the sacrifice of himself" (Heb. 9:26, NIV). It calls all persons to participate fully, through cruciform faith, in Christ's victory. This is grace-enabled justification-regeneration, sanctification, and mission. It is unending co-crucifixion and co-resurrection. It is new creation—reconciliation, healing, and wholeness. It is divine light scattering the darkness. It is grace abounding more than sin ever could. It is invitation to Christian discipleship and mission. And it is normative discipleship made possible by the will of the Father and the atoning work of Messiah Jesus and made effectual through the indwelling Holy Spirit.

Biblical scholarship has never provided a clearer and more urgent mandate for understanding and declaring Christian holiness as the norm of Christian discipleship than today. This gold mine must be explored and extensively excavated through study, proclamation, and practice, "in order that [we] may gain Christ and be found in him, not having a righteousness of [our] own, based on law, but that which is through faith in Christ, the righteousness from God that depends on faith; that [we] may know him and the power of his resurrection, and may share his sufferings, becoming like him in his death, that if possible [we] may attain the resurrection from the dead" (Phil. 3:8-11).

John R. Stott says this goal is impossible except through the indwelling Holy Spirit, who from the inside changes Christians into the likeness of Christ. To make his point, Stott borrows from Archbishop William Temple's (1881–1944) use of Shakespeare. "It is no good giving me a play like *Hamlet* or *King Lear* and telling me to write a play like that. Shakespeare could do it—I can't. And it is no good showing me a life like the life of Jesus and telling me to live a life like that. Jesus could do it—I can't. But if the genius of Shakespeare could come and live in me, then I could write plays like this. And if the Spirit could come into me, then I could live a life like [Jesus's]." The Father's purpose is to make us Christlike. He does this by way of the Holy Spirit dwelling in us. "In other words, [Christlikeness] is . . . Trinitarian."[45]

Everything the Father through the Son and by the Holy Spirit offers his people must, by grace through faith, be claimed and practiced now. That is the majestic call of the New Testament. Response should be decisive and determinative, punctual and unending—missional.

> *Refining Fire, go thro' my heart;*
> *Illuminate my soul.*
> *Scatter Thy life thro' ev'ry part,*
> *And sanctify the whole.*[46]

---

45. John R. Stott, "The Model: Becoming More Like Christ," John Stott's final address, delivered at the Keswick Convention, July 17, 2007, *Knowing and Doing*, Fall 2009, http://www.cslewisinstitute.org/Becoming_More_Like_Christ _Stott.

46. Charles Wesley, "Jesus, Thine All-Victorious Love," in *Sing to the Lord* (Kansas City: Lillenas, 1993), no. 500.

TEN

Divine Gift
Forgiveness That Leads to Eternal Life

Forgiveness is arguably the most challenging topic associated with sin and Christian faith. We usually have little difficulty accepting God's forgiveness. But forgiving those we judge to be undeserving can cause "religious heartburn." The latter includes the thorny topic of forgiveness as it relates to justice.

　　While serving as a seminary professor, I also served as the chaplain for a women's "safe house," where traumatized and often brutalized women and children were offered shelter and protection. I have looked into the fearful, wondering faces of women and children marked by agonizing memories of abuse, but with no discernible futures. They were afraid to exit the safe house for fear the cycle of abuse would resume. Moreover, they had no place to go. Coming from my comfortable position as a professor, I was supposed to offer some measure of hope and peace amid emotional chaos and then return with a measure of emotional stability to teach Christian ethics to future ministers, while internally roiled by anger and unresolved questions.

　　I have yet to see a book that neatly answers all questions associated with forgiveness. No matter how thoroughly we try, some questions remain inadequately answered. We must not fixate on "answerable" questions and leave problem areas unaddressed.

We will focus on three of Jesus's parables and part of the Lord's Prayer. Sin's nature is to wound, enslave, disrupt, alienate, build and fortify divisive walls, destroy institutions, generate suspicion, and provide ironclad reasons for making offenses permanent. Forgiveness and reconciliation are two of sin's most formidable enemies. The kingdom of evil mounts a vigorous defense.

The Compassionate Employer and Laborers in the Vineyard (Matt. 20:1–16)

New Testament scholar Kenneth Bailey says this parable is filled with questions, surprises, and passions.[1] It reveals the character of God and hence the character he desires to cultivate in Christians. The parable tells us that God is not bound by the restrictions our cultural calculations usually require as norms for relationships. On the surface, the parable concerns equitable wages. But hiring practices and pay scales are not its point. It has wide-ranging applications.

"The kingdom of heaven is like a householder who went out early in the morning to hire laborers for his vineyard" (Matt. 20:1). They began work at 6:00 a.m. and were promised a denarius for the day. This was considered a living wage. The owner continued hiring others throughout the day: 9:00 a.m., 12:00 p.m., 3:00 p.m., and 5:00 p.m. The last hire was close to quitting time.

When evening came, the householder instructed his steward to begin paying the 5:00 p.m. laborers first—one denarius. The hearts of the 6:00 a.m. laborers must have leaped with anticipation. But contrary to expectations, the owner paid those who had worked since sunrise no more than he paid the 5:00 p.m. hires—one denarius! The 6:00 a.m. laborers were outraged. Kenneth Bailey says they

---

1. Kenneth E. Bailey, *Jesus through Middle Eastern Eyes* (Downers Grove, IL: IVP Academic, 2008), 357.

"could not tolerate grace. You have made the unemployed scum, whom no one else wanted, equal to us!"[2]

What the householder did was *unfair by normal standards*. An explanation was demanded. Surprisingly, instead of explaining things according to human norms, the householder turned everything upside down. He appealed to his own sovereignty. "Am I not allowed to do what I choose with what belongs to me? Or do you begrudge my generosity?" (v. 15). The answer to both questions is yes. You are free to do what you choose with what you own. And yes, we do begrudge your generosity.

"Grace," says Kenneth Bailey, is not only "amazing" but, for many, also "infuriating."[3] Many quickly side with the 6:00 a.m. workers. "Fair is fair!"

The parable can apply to the Gentiles who came late to God's kingdom but were admitted on the same basis as the Jews who had labored since the day they left Egypt (Rom. 9:22-33). It can also apply to God's forgiveness. By human standards, some are more deserving than others. So when God freely forgives and reconciles sinners who haven't been as morally and religiously scrupulous as we, we howl in protest. If God were just, if he were to mete out forgiveness as "fairness" requires, there would be a clear demarcation between payment for the 6:00 a.m. hires and the latecomers.

But there is a subtle twist in the parable. Many of us quickly identify with the 6:00 a.m. folk. However, the New Testament says we are all 5:00 p.m. laborers. "We all, like sheep, have gone astray, each of us has turned to our own way; and the LORD has laid on him the iniquity of us all" (Isa. 53:6, NIV). "But God demonstrates his own love for us in this: While we were still sinners, Christ died for us" (Rom. 5:8, NIV).

---

2. Ibid., 361.
3. Ibid.

We begin to understand forgiveness by recognizing we can't deserve it. Forgiveness can be given, but never earned. The notion of earning forgiveness, either from God or from some person, comes at the expense of minimizing the offense committed and exaggerating our own worth. "Earning" never rises above self-justification. And it always depreciates the one offended.

As Christians, we should begin, and continue to believe, we all began at 5:00 p.m. Paul told the Corinthians, "For I am the least of the apostles, unfit to be called an apostle, because I persecuted the church of God. But by the grace of God I am what I am, and his grace toward me was not in vain" (1 Cor. 15:9-10*a*). The parable of the laborers forces two unavoidable questions. *First*, Do I want to be associated with and defined by a God who behaves this way? *Second*, Am I willing to become his representative in the world?

Kenneth Bailey says the parable lacks a conclusion. What happened to the complaining employees? Did they take their pay and leave, finally satisfied with the householder's actions? Or did they continue shouting at him, demanding more? Were they ever reconciled to the householder, who was not only just but also merciful, gracious, and compassionate?[4]

The Unforgiving Servant (Matt. 18:21-35)

The parable of the unforgiving servant is a parable of the kingdom. It is a literary gem. Its fifteen verses are complete with intriguing characters, supporting actors, surprising twists, irony, anger, and pointed applications. This is the story of the God who freely forgives sinners. Peter asks a question that seems to need only a simple answer. "Lord,

---

4. Ibid., 357.

how often shall my brother sin against me, and I forgive him? As many as seven times?" (Matt. 18:21).

Instead of answering numerically, Jesus answers qualitatively. Rather than speak from within the confines of Jewish legalism and the Greco-Roman world, Jesus speaks about the kingdom of God. Immediately we realize we have entered a world different from Peter's quantitative question.

Jesus tells of a king who wished to settle accounts with his servants. The time had come to pay up. One by one they came forward. So far, we are still in a *quantitative* world. Then the discourse radically changes. Jesus shifts from *quantity* to *quality*. A debtor came before the king. He owed the king ten thousand talents. This is equivalent to 150,000 years of wages! Payment is impossible. Nevertheless, the king commands, "Pay up!"

Lamely casting about for something to say, the debtor fell on his knees and absurdly implored the king, "Lord, have patience with me, and I will pay you everything" (v. 26). Might this be the most humorous verse in the Bible? A mortal proposes to pay off a debt equivalent to 150,000 years of wages.

Now comes the apex of the story. "And out of pity for him the Lord of that servant released him and forgave him the debt" (v. 27). The forgiveness received should have transformed the debtor. He should have viewed himself and others through the lens of having been forgiven an incomprehensible debt.

The terrain shifts as we return from the *incalculable* to the *calculable*. "That same servant, as he went out, came upon one of his fellow servants who owed him a hundred denarii; and seizing him by the throat he said, 'Pay what you owe.' So his fellow servant fell down and besought him, 'Have patience with me, and I will pay you.' He refused and went and put him in prison till he should pay the debt" (vv. 28-29). The second servant used the same words as the first. The second servant "fell" on his knees just as the first servant had.

This was the first servant's opportunity to demonstrate what he had learned. He failed miserably. What had happened to him vertically a few minutes earlier was not permitted to enter his horizontal world. The fellow servant owed one hundred days of wages. This was not an insignificant amount. However, it was manageable. The fellow servant was willing to pay everything, if only a payment schedule could be arranged.

Instead, the first servant employed all the powers of the law to exact punishment. The law permitted him to throw the entire family into prison. Here is the irony. The first servant was determined to keep the family in prison until the father could pay the entire debt. How could the man hope to pay the debt when all routes for doing so had been denied? That is the nature of unforgiveness: "Lock them up until . . ." In the words of N. T. Wright, the first servant was determined "to make the moral universe rotate around the fulcrum of [his] own sulk."[5] In the process, he placed himself and his fellow servant "in prison."

The problem with the servant's double standard was that the forgiving king would permit no such bifurcation. Upon hearing the news, he hauled the unforgiving servant back into his presence. Now the king's disposition has completely changed. "'You wicked servant! I forgave you all that debt because you besought me; and should not you have had mercy on your fellow servant, as I had mercy on you?' And in anger his lord delivered him to the jailers, till he should pay all his debt" (vv. 32-34).

In effect, Jesus said, "My Father respects your preferred standard." "So also my heavenly Father will do to every one

5. N. T. Wright, *Evil and the Justice of God* (Downers Grove, IL: IVP Books, 2006), 160.

of you, if you do not forgive your brother from your heart" (v. 35). N. T. Wright said Jesus was telling his disciples the long-awaited "new age is here, the age of forgiveness, and that his people are to embody it."[6]

R. T. Kendall, pastor of Westminster Chapel in London, England, for twenty-five years, says that "most of us have had times in our lives when we have been pushed to our limits as to how much we are called to forgive." He includes himself by admitting, "I . . . was unable to forgive for much of my life."[7] Kendall tells of an instance in which he had been deeply hurt. The wound affected almost every part of his ministry, including his sense of self-worth. "There I was in the ministry of the Lord Jesus, filled with so much hurt and bitterness that I could hardly fulfill my duties. . . . I thought, God fully [understands] and sympathizes with my particular circumstances."[8]

Dr. Kendall told a friend about the offense, expecting sympathy. The friend responded, "R. T., you must totally forgive them. Release them, and you will be set free."[9] It was the hardest thing Kendall had ever tried to do. "I had to make an important decision: which do I prefer—the peace or the bitterness? I couldn't have it both ways."[10]

Kendall obeyed the voice of the Lord spoken through his honest friend. As he began to forgive, "an unexpected blessing" came over him. "A peace came into my heart that I hadn't felt in years. It was wonderful. I had forgotten

---

6. Ibid., 155. Wright says, "The faculty we have for receiving forgiveness and the faculty we have for granting forgiveness are one and the same thing. If we open the one, we shall open the other. If we slam the door on the one, we slam the door on the other" (159).

7. R. T. Kendall, *Total Forgiveness*, rev. ed. (Lake Mary, FL: Charisma House, 2007), 2.

8. Ibid., 3.

9. Ibid., 4.

10. Ibid., 5.

what it was like."[11] Kendall doesn't make forgiveness easy. "I found I had to carry out that decision by a daily commitment to forgive those who hurt me, to forgive them totally."[12]

The Lord's Prayer (Matthew 6:9-13)

Pope Benedict XVI says the Lord's Prayer "aims to form our being, to train us in the inner attitude of Jesus. . . . It is a Trinitarian prayer: We pray with Christ through the Holy Spirit to the Father."[13]

Matthew's version of the Lord's Prayer has six petitions (cf. Luke 11:2-4).[14] We will focus on the fifth: "Forgive us our debts, as we also have forgiven our debtors" (Matt. 6:12).

There is a recurring need for God's forgiveness of us and for our forgiveness of others. Forgiveness should not be considered

a grand dramatic act that occurs at the beginning of the Christian pilgrimage of faith, but as a daily need. Each day the faithful need to ask God to pick up the broken pieces of their lives and restore to them the joy of their salvation. . . . Unless people are able to forgive one another and to seek God's forgiveness, they are unable to live together. The healing that comes from forgiveness makes it possible for the faithful to continue their pilgrimage as a community.[15]

---

11. Ibid., 4.

12. Ibid., 5-6.

13. Benedict XVI, *Jesus of Nazareth: From the Baptism in the Jordan to the Transfiguration* (New York: Image, 2007), 132, 135.

14. The number of petitions is not agreed upon. The Lord's Prayer falls into two parts. The first relates to God; the second to humans. After the opening invocation there are three petitions concerning God's glory (Matt. 6:9-10). Depending on how one treats verse 13, the total number of petitions is either six or seven.

15. Bailey, *Jesus through Middle Eastern Eyes*, 126.

Bailey explains that "biblical forgiveness does not mean 'Never mind.' Offering forgiveness does not dictate that injustice must be tolerated. . . . Those who pray [the Lord's Prayer] are not affirming, 'Injustice can continue, it doesn't . . . matter. We are willing to ignore injustice to ourselves and others.'"[16] Desmond Tutu teaches, "Forgiveness is not cheap, is not [effortless]. It is costly. Reconciliation is not an easy option. It cost God the death of his Son."[17]

As Amos and Micah knew, forgiveness must be understood in relationship to justice. Forgiveness of others is seldom automatic. It can be complex, take time, and involve pain. But the disposition to forgive, to permit the Holy Spirit to effect an inner change that makes forgiveness possible and responsible, must be present for the Lord's Prayer to have meaning. Rejecting a willingness to forgive entails rejecting the God who forgives.

No Future without Forgiveness[18]

N. T. Wright speaks of forgiveness as part of the Christian stewardship of the costly forgiveness God in Christ offers. Forgiveness is "part of the stewardly vocation of genuine human existence, bringing God's order into the minds and hearts of others and thereby enabling people both to worship the true God and to serve his continuing purposes."[19]

Felicia Sanders and Nadine Collier knew and displayed the stewardship Wright commends. On the evening of June 17, 2015, during the regular Wednesday evening Bible study in the Mother Emanuel African Methodist

---

16. Ibid., 126-27.

17. Desmond Tutu, 1998 Mollegen Lecture, *Virginia Seminary Journal* (January 1999), quoted in Rutledge, *Crucifixion*, 115.

18. The phrase comes from Desmond Tutu, *No Future without Forgiveness* (New York: Doubleday, 1999).

19. Wright, *Evil and the Justice of God*, 141.

Episcopal Church in Charleston, South Carolina, twenty-one-year-old white supremacist Dylann Roof sat for a while as a welcomed guest. Then, without warning, he stood and proceeded to murder nine people, including Pastor Clementa C. Pinckney. Pastor Pinckney was also a respected South Carolina state senator. Roof's youngest victim was twenty-six-year-old Tywanza Sanders. As Roof proceeded to kill, Tywanza died while trying to shield his eighty-seven-year-old great-aunt Susie Jackson. "You don't have to do this," Tywanza told Roof and then moved into the line of fire.[20]

Tywanza's mother, Felicia Sanders, survived the murderous rampage by playing dead. At Roof's bond hearing on June 19, 2015, Felicia placed the death of her son in simple terms. "We welcomed you Wednesday night in our Bible study with welcome arms. . . . Tywanza Sanders was my son. But Tywanza Sanders was my hero. . . . May God have mercy on you."[21] Nadine Collier, the daughter of Ethel Lance, one of the nine victims, told Roof: "I will never be able to hold her again, but I forgive you. And have mercy on your soul. You hurt me. You hurt a lot of people but God forgives you, and I forgive you."[22]

N. T. Wright offers six principles that can inform and guide the stewardship of forgiveness.

First, when we forgive someone, we are no longer conditioned by the wrong they have committed. This is true

---

20. Ed Pilkington, "'He Was My Hero': Charleston Mother Hails 26-Year-Old Killed Shielding Victims," *The Guardian* (US edition), June 19, 2015, https://www.theguardian.com/world/2015/jun/19/hero-charleston-church-shooting-mother-shielding-others.

21. Mark Berman, "'I Forgive You.' Relatives of Charleston Church Shooting Victims Address Dylann Roof," *Washington Post*, June 19, 2015, https://www.washingtonpost.com/news/post-nation/wp/2015/06/19/i-forgive-you-relatives-of-charleston-church-victims-address-dylann-roof/.

22. *Atlanta Journal-Constitution*, "Emotions Run High at Dylann Roof's Bond Hearing," June 19, 2015, https://www.ajc.com/news/national/emotions-run-high-dylann-roof-bond-hearing/EvnEnfqJeQikrMG5bQ3fDM/.

even if the offending party will not accept forgiveness and chooses to remain in a state of conflict.[23]

Second, God calls us to be people of forgiveness now because that is how we will live in our future resurrected life. "Just as physical decay and death will have no power over our resurrection bodies, so the moral decay and dissolution threatened by the persistent presence of evil . . . will have no power over our emotional and moral lives in the world to come."[24] As much as possible, the vision of resurrected life, of God's future world, should shape our world now.

Third, forgiveness must not be confused with tolerance. We take evil seriously. "It means a settled determination to name evil and to shame it; without that, there is, after all, nothing to forgive." Forgiveness does not mean the offense committed against me was insignificant or that it did not actually happen. It was significant and it did happen. Forgiveness does not entail that we just let people get away with evil and injustice. It cannot be ignored as irrelevant. "Forgiveness is looking hard at the fact that [the offense did happen] and [then] making a conscious . . . decision of the moral will to set it aside so that it doesn't [remain] a barrier between us."

Fourth, forgiveness means we are determined to do all we can to restore relationship with the offending party once the injustice has been dealt with.[25]

Fifth, "forgiveness means we have settled it in our minds that we shall not allow . . . evil to determine the sort of people" we will become. "That is what forgiveness is all about. It is tough: tough to do, tough to receive—and tough also in the sense that once it's really happened, forgiveness

23. Wright, *Evil and the Justice of God,* 141.
24. Ibid., 142-43.
25. Ibid., 157.

is strong, unlike a soggy tolerance which merely takes the line of least resistance."[26]

Sixth, learning to forgive oneself is an essential part of God's forgiveness. This can be more difficult than forgiving others. But fully responding to the gospel of Jesus Christ includes opening our hearts as wide as possible and learning how to forgive ourselves without minimizing the wrong we have committed.[27] But if God forgives us, and if we have made restitution with others as much as is wise and possible, "then it is part of living an authentically Christian life that you learn to forgive yourself as well."[28]

---

26. Ibid.
27. Ibid., 162-63.
28. Ibid., 163.

Bibliography

Achtemeier, Paul J., Joel B. Green, and Marianne M. Thompson. *Introducing the New Testament: Its Literature and Theology*. Grand Rapids: Eerdmans, 2001.

Africa Adventures. "Large Elephant 'Ngonyama' Road Block." YouTube Video, 6:03. June 13, 2018. https://www.youtube.com /watch?v=hMbYnol1iFQ.

Ambrose. *On the Holy Spirit*. In vol. 10 of *Nicene and Post-Nicene Fathers* (series II). Edited by Philip Schaff and Henry Wace. Reprint of 1896 edition. Christian Classics Ethereal Library (CCEL). https://ccel.org/ccel/s/schaff/npnf210/cache/npnf210.pdf.

Anderson, Bernhard W. *Understanding the Old Testament*. 3rd ed. Englewood Cliffs, NJ: Prentice-Hall, 1975.

Anderson, Gary A. *Christian Doctrine and the Old Testament: Theology in the Service of Biblical Exegesis*. Grand Rapids: Baker Academic, 2017.

———. *Sin: A History*. New Haven, CT: Yale University Press, 2010.

Atlanta Journal-Constitution. "Emotions Run High at Dylann Roof's Bond Hearing." June 19, 2015. https://www.ajc.com/news /national/emotions-run-high-dylann-roof-bond-hearing /EvnEnfqJeQikrMG5bQ3fDM/.

Augustine. *Anti-Pelagian Writings*. In vol. 5 of *Nicene and Post-Nicene Fathers* (series I). Edited by Philip Schaff. Reprint of 1887 edition. CCEL. https://www.ccel.org/ccel/schaff/npnf105.

———. *The City of God*. In vol. 2 of *Nicene and Post-Nicene Fathers* (series I). Edited by Philip Schaff. Reprint of 1886 edition. CCEL. https://www.ccel.org/ccel/schaff/npnf102.pdf.

———. *Confessions and Enchiridion*. Translated and edited by Albert C. Outler. Philadelphia: Westminster Press, 1955. Reprint, CCEL. http://www.ccel.org/ccel/augustine/confessions.pdf.

———. *On the Holy Trinity*. In vol. 3 of *Nicene and Post-Nicene Fathers* (series I). Edited by Philip Schaff. Reprint of 1887 edition. CCEL. https://www.ccel.org/ccel/schaff/npnf103.pdf.

———. *Retractationes*. Translated by Meredith Freeman Eller. Boston: Boston University Graduate School, 1946. Internet Archive. https://archive.org/details/retractationesof00elle.

Bailey, Kenneth E. *Jesus through Middle Eastern Eyes*. Downers Grove, IL: IVP Academic, 2008.

Barron, Robert. "The Gatherer." Ch. 4 in *The Priority of Christ: Toward a Postliberal Catholicism*. Grand Rapids: Brazos Press, 2007. https://www.google.com/books/edition/_/zrdzBQAAQBAJ?hl=en&gbpv=1.

Barth, Karl. *Church Dogmatics*. Vol. 2, *The Doctrine of God*, pt. 1. Edinburgh: T. and T. Clark International, 2004.

———. *Church Dogmatics*. Vol. 4, *The Doctrine of Reconciliation*, pt. 1. Edinburgh: T. and T. Clark International, 2004.

Bell, Daniel. *The Cultural Contradictions of Capitalism*. New York: Basic Books, 1996.

Benedict XVI. *Jesus of Nazareth: From the Baptism in the Jordan to the Transfiguration*. New York: Image, 2007.

Berger, Peter L. *The Many Altars of Modernity: Toward a Paradigm for Religion in a Pluralist Age*. Boston: Walter de Gruyter, 2014.

Berkhof, Hendrikus. *Christ and the Powers*. Translated by John H. Yoder. Scottdale, PA: Herald Press, 1977.

Berman, Mark. "'I Forgive You.' Relatives of Charleston Church Shooting Victims Address Dylann Roof." *Washington Post*, June 19, 2015. https://www.washingtonpost.com/news/post-nation/wp/2015/06/19/i-forgive-you-relatives-of-charleston-church-victims-address-dylann-roof/.

Bonhoeffer, Dietrich. *The Cost of Discipleship*. New York: Touchstone Book, 1995.

Braaten, Carl E. "God in Public Life: Rehabilitating the 'Orders of Creation.'" *First Things* (December 1990). https://www.firstthings.com/article/1990/12/god-in-public-life-rehabilitating-the-orders-of-creation.

Brown, Colin, ed. *The New International Dictionary of New Testament Theology*. Vol. 3. Grand Rapids: Zondervan, 1979.

Brown, William P. *The Seven Pillars of Creation: The Bible, Science, and the Ecology of Wonder*. Oxford, UK: Oxford University Press, 2010.

Brueggemann, Walter. *Reverberations of Faith: A Theological Handbook of Old Testament Themes*. Louisville, KY: Westminster John Knox Press, 2002.

Brunner, Peter. "Commitment to the Lutheran Confession: What Does It Mean Today?" *The Springfielder* 33, no. 3 (December 1969): 4-14. http://www.ctsfw.net/media/pdfs/brunnercommitmentto confessions.pdf.

Caird, G. B. *The Language and Imagery of the Bible*. Philadelphia: Westminster, 1980.

———. *Principalities and Powers: A Study in Pauline Theology*. Eugene, OR: Wipf and Stock, 2003.

Calvin, John. *Commentary on Romans*. Translated and edited by John Owen. Edinburgh: Calvin Translation Society, 1849. Reprint, CCEL. https://www.ccel.org/ccel/calvin/calcom38.pdf.

———. *The Institutes of the Christian Religion*. Translated by Henry Beveridge. Edinburgh: Calvin Translation Society, 1845. Reprint, CCEL. http://www.ccel.org/ccel/calvin/institutes.pdf.

Crossman, Ashley. "The Concept of Social Structure in Sociology." ThoughtCo. Updated June 28, 2019. https://www.thoughtco .com/social-structure-defined-3026594.

Cyprian. Treatise I of *The Treatises of Cyprian*, "On the Unity of the Church." In vol. 5 of *Ante-Nicene Fathers*. Edited by A. Cleveland Coxe. Reprint of 1885 edition. CCEL. http://www.ccel.org/ccel /schaff/anf05.pdf.

"Despised Trades according to the Mishnah and the Talmud." BYU Studies. http://byustudies.byu.edu/wp-content/uploads /2021/02/3-10.pdf (accessed July 22, 2021).

Dodd, C. H. *The Interpretation of the Fourth Gospel*. Cambridge, UK: Cambridge University Press, 1970.

Donne, John. "Meditation XVII." In *Devotions upon Emergent Occasions*. 1624. Reprint, Ann Arbor, MI: University of Michigan Press, 1959; Project Gutenberg, 2007. https://www.gutenberg.org /files/23772/23772-h/23772-h.htm.

Dostoyevsky, Fyodor. "Rebellion." Ch. 4 in bk. 5 of *The Brothers Karamazov*. 1880. Translated by Constance Garnett. New York: Lowell Press, 1912; reprint, Project Gutenberg, 2009. https:// www.gutenberg.org/files/28054/28054-h/28054-h.htm.

Dunson, Ben C. *Individual and Community in Paul's Letter to the Romans*. Tübingen, DEU: Mohr Siebeck, 2012.

Farr, Thomas F. "Diplomacy and Persecution in China." *First Things* (May 2019): 29-35. https://www.firstthings.com/article /2019/05/diplomacy-and-persecution-in-china.

Gorman, Michael J. *Becoming the Gospel: Paul, Participation, and Mission.* Grand Rapids: Eerdmans, 2015.

———. *The Death of the Messiah and the Birth of the New Covenant.* Eugene, OR: Cascade Books, 2014.

———. *Inhabiting the Cruciform God: Kenosis, Justification, and Theosis in Paul's Narrative Soteriology.* Grand Rapids: Eerdmans, 2009.

Greathouse, William M. *Wholeness in Christ: Toward a Biblical Theology of Holiness.* Kansas City: Beacon Hill Press of Kansas City, 1998.

Hays, Richard B. *Echoes of Scripture in the Gospels.* Waco, TX: Baylor University Press, 2016.

———. *Reading Backwards: Figural Christology and the Fourfold Gospel Witness.* 2014. Reprint, Waco, TX: Baylor University Press, 2016.

Imbelli, Robert P. *Rekindling the Christic Imagination.* Collegeville, MN: Liturgical Press, 2014.

Irenaeus. *The Demonstration of the Apostolic Preaching.* Sec. 29. Translated and edited by Armitage Robinson. London: Society for Promoting Christian Knowledge, 1920. Reprint, CCEL. https:// www.ccel.org/ccel/irenaeus/demonstr.pdf.

Jenson, Robert W. *Systematic Theology.* Vol. 1, *The Triune God.* Oxford, UK: Oxford University Press, 1997.

———. *Systematic Theology.* Vol. 2, *The Works of God.* Oxford, UK: Oxford University Press, 1999.

Johnson, Luke Timothy. *The Real Jesus.* San Francisco: HarperSanFrancisco, 1996.

———. *The Writings of the New Testament: An Interpretation.* Minneapolis: Fortress Press, 1986.

Jung, C. G. *The Archetypes and the Collective Unconscious.* Vol. 9 (pt. 1) of *The Collected Works of C. G. Jung.* Princeton, NJ: Princeton University Press, 1981.

Kant, Immanuel. "The Christian Religion as a Natural Religion," bk. 4, pt 1, sec. 1, of *Religion within the Limits of Reason Alone.* 1793. Translated by Theodore M. Greene and Hoyt H. Hudson. New York: HarperOne, 2008.

———. "What Is Enlightenment?, 1784." Internet Modern History Sourcebook. Fordham University. https://sourcebooks.fordham .edu/mod/kant-whatis.asp.

Kärkkäinen, Veli-Matti. *One with God: Salvation as Deification and Justification.* Collegeville, MN: Liturgical Press, 2004.

Kendall, R. T. *Total Forgiveness*. Rev. ed. Lake Mary, FL: Charisma House, 2007.

Kierkegaard, Søren. "The Sickness unto Death." In *A Kierkegaard Anthology*. Edited by Robert Bretall. Princeton, NJ: Princeton University Press, 1946.

——. "Training in Christianity." In *A Kierkegaard Anthology*. Edited by Robert Bretall. Princeton, NJ: Princeton University Press, 1946.

King, Martin Luther, Jr. "Letter from a Birmingham Jail." April 16, 1963. The Martin Luther King Jr. Research and Education Institute. Stanford University. http://okra.stanford.edu/transcription /document_images/undecided/630416-019.pdf.

Luther, Martin. *A Commentary on St. Paul's Epistle to the Galatians*. 1535. Translated by Theodore Graebner. Grand Rapids: Zondervan, 1949. Reprint, CCEL. https://www.ccel.org/ccel/luther /galatians.pdf.

——. "Preface to the Epistle of St. Paul to the Romans." 1522. In *Martin Luther: Selections from His Writings*. Edited by John Dillenberger. Garden City, NY: Doubleday, 1961.

MacIntyre, Alasdair. *After Virtue*. Notre Dame, IN: University of Notre Dame Press, 1984.

Meyer, Paul W. *The Word in This World: Essays in New Testament Exegesis and Theology*, ed. John T. Carroll. Louisville, KY: Westminster John Knox Press, 2004.

Montaigne, Michel de. "Of Custom, and That We Should Not Easily Change a Law Received." Ch. 22 in bk. 1 of *Essays of Michel De Montaigne*. Translated by Charles Cotton. 1877. Reprint, Project Gutenberg, 2006. http://www.gutenberg.org/files/3600/3600-h /3600-h.htm#link2HCH0022.

Nessan, Craig L. "The Relation of Justification and Sanctification in the Lutheran Tradition." Ch. 5 in *All Things Needed for Godliness: A Portrait of Holiness among Christian Traditions*. Edited by Al Truesdale. Kansas City: Foundry Publishing, 2020.

Newman, John Henry. "General Answer to Mr. Kingsley." Pt. 7 of *Apologia pro Vita Sua*. London: Longman, Green, Longman, Roberts, and Green, 1864. Reprint, CCEL. http://www.ccel.org/ccel /newman/apologia.pdf.

Neyrey, Jerome H. "The Idea of Purity in Mark's Gospel." University of Notre Dame. https://www3.nd.edu/~jneyrey1/Purity-Mark.html.

——. "The Social Location of Paul: Education as the Key." University of Notre Dame. https://www3.nd.edu/~jneyrey1/social -location.htm.

Neyrey, Jerome H., and Eric C. Stewart, eds. *The Social World of the New Testament: Insights and Models.* Peabody, MA: Hendrickson, 2008.

Nietzsche, Friedrich. "The Higher Man." Ch. 73 in pt. 4 of *Thus Spake Zarathustra.* 1883. Translated by Thomas Common. New York: Macmillan, 1916; reprint, Project Gutenberg, 2008. https://www.gutenberg.org/files/1998/1998-h/1998-h.htm#link2H_4_0052.

Novak, Michael. *The Spirit of Democratic Capitalism.* New York: Touchstone, 1982.

O'Connor, Flannery. "A Good Man Is Hard to Find." In *Flannery O'Connor: The Complete Stories.* New York: Farrar, Straus and Giroux, 1971.

———. "Revelation." In *Flannery O'Connor: The Complete Stories.* New York: Farrar, Straus and Giroux, 1971.

Otto, Rudolph. *The Idea of the Holy.* 1917. Translated by John W. Harvey. Oxford, UK: Oxford University Press, 1936; first published 1923.

Peck, M. Scott. *The People of the Lie.* New York: Simon and Schuster, 1983.

Pilkington, Ed. "'He Was My Hero': Charleston Mother Hails 26-Year-Old Killed Shielding Victims." *Guardian* (US edition), June 19, 2015. https://www.theguardian.com/world/2015/jun/19/hero-charleston-church-shooting-mother-shielding-others.

Polley, Max E. "The Place of Henry Wheeler Robinson among Old Testament Scholars." *The Baptist Quarterly* 24, no. 6 (April 1972): 271-83. https://biblicalstudies.org.uk/pdf/bq/24-6_271.pdf.

Rahner, Karl. *The Trinity.* Translated by Joseph Donceel. New York: Herder and Herder, 1970.

Ricoeur, Paul. *The Symbolism of Evil.* Translated by Emerson Buchanan. Boston: Beacon Press, 1967.

Riley, Alexander. "A Religion of Activism." *First Things* (April 2019): 9-11. https://www.firstthings.com/article/2019/04/a-religion-of-activism.

Royal, Robert. "Our Tower of Babel." The Catholic Thing, June 3, 2019. https://www.thecatholicthing.org/2019/06/03/our-tower-of-babel/?utm_source=The+Catholic+Thing+Daily&utm_campaign=5272111e67-EMAIL_CAMPAIGN_2018_12_07_01_02_COPY_01&utm_medium=email&utm_term=0_769a14e16a-5272111e67-244109025.

Rutledge, Fleming. *The Crucifixion: Understanding the Death of Jesus Christ*. 2015. Reprint, Grand Rapids: Eerdmans, 2017.

Severson, Eric R. *Scandalous Obligation: Rethinking Christian Responsibility*. Kansas City: Beacon Hill Press of Kansas City, 2011.

Shedd, William G. T. Introductory essay to *On the Holy Trinity*, by Augustine, 7-17. In vol. 3 of *Nicene and Post-Nicene Fathers* (series I). Edited by Philip Schaff. Reprint of 1887 edition. CCEL. https://www.ccel.org/ccel/schaff/npnf103.pdf.

Sindreu, Jon, and Sarah Kent. "Why It's So Hard to Be an 'Ethical' Investor." *Wall Street Journal*, September 1, 2018.

Stott, John R. "The Model: Becoming More like Christ." John Stott's final address, delivered at the Keswick Convention, July 17, 2007. *Knowing and Doing*, Fall 2009. http://www.cslewisinstitute.org/Becoming_More_Like_Christ_Stott.

Taylor, Charles. *A Secular Age*. Cambridge, MA: Belknap Press of Harvard University Press, 2018.

Taylor, John V. *The Christlike God*. London: SCM Press, 2004.

Tutu, Desmond. *No Future without Forgiveness*. New York: Doubleday, 1999.

Varughese, Alex. Telephone conversation with author, November 28, 2018. Mount Vernon Nazarene College, Mount Vernon, OH.

Volf, Miroslav. *Exclusion and Embrace: A Theological Exploration of Identity, Otherness, and Reconciliation*. Nashville: Abingdon Press, 1996.

Wainwright, Geoffrey. *Doxology: The Praise of God in Worship, Doctrine, and Life*. New York: Oxford University Press, 1980.

Walton, John H. *The Lost World of Genesis One: Ancient Cosmology and the Origins Debate*. Downers Grove, IL: IVP Academic, 2009.

Ware, Kallistos. *The Orthodox Way*. Crestwood, NY: St. Vladimir's Seminary Press, 1979.

Watson, David. "The Ontology of Principalities and Powers." *Wesleyan Theological Journal* 56, no. 1 (Spring 2021): 52-53.

Weigel, George. *Evangelical Catholicism: Deep Reform in the 21st-Century Church*. New York: Basic Books, 2013.

Wilson, E. O. *The Creation: An Appeal to Save Life on Earth*. New York: W. W. Norton and Company, 2006.

Wink, Walter. *Naming the Powers: The Language of Power in the New Testament*. Philadelphia: Fortress Press, 1984.

Wirzba, Norman. *Way of Love: Recovering the Heart of Christianity*. New York: HarperOne, 2016.

Witherington, Ben, III. "Does Romans 7 Teach That Christians Will Continue Sinning?" YouTube Video, 8:47, posted by "Seedbed." July 29, 2014. https://www.youtube.com/watch?reload =9&v=aBXYp7cMblM.

————. "The Freedom of God and the Free Will of Human Beings." *Ben Witherington* (blog), June 10, 2008. http://benwitherington .blogspot.com/2008/06/freedom-of-god-and-free-will-of -human.html.

Woodward, C. Vann. *The Strange Career of Jim Crow*. New York: Oxford University Press, 1955.

Wright, Christopher J. H. *The Mission of God: Unlocking the Bible's Grand Narrative*. Downers Grove, IL: IVP Academic, 2006.

Wright, N. T. *The Challenge of Jesus: Rediscovering Who Jesus Was and Is*. Downers Grove, IL: InterVarsity Press, 1999.

————. *The Day the Revolution Began: Reconsidering the Meaning of Jesus's Crucifixion*. San Francisco: HarperOne, 2016.

————. "Discerning the Dawn: Knowing God in the New Creation." YouTube Video, 1:12:15, posted by "fleetwd1." May 8, 2017. https://www.youtube.com/watch?v=ZGX4EcJFupQ.

————. *Evil and the Justice of God*. Downers Grove, IL: IVP Books, 2006.

————. *Paul: A Biography*. San Francisco: HarperOne, 2018.

Wright, N. T., and Michael F. Bird. *The New Testament in Its World*. Grand Rapids: Zondervan Academic, 2019.

Yancey, Philip. *What's So Amazing about Grace?* Study Guide Edition. Grand Rapids: Zondervan, 1998.

www.ingramcontent.com/pod-product-compliance
Lightning Source LLC
Chambersburg PA
CBHW070038100426
42740CB00013B/2721